M

Fr

PORTABLE

Turks & Caicos

1st Edition

by Alexis Lipsitz Flippin

Here's what critics say about Frommer's:

"Amazingly easy to use. Very portable, very complete."

—*Booklist*

"Detailed, accurate, and easy-to-read information for all price ranges."

—*Glamour Magazine*

BICENTENNIAL
1807
WILEY
2007
BICENTENNIAL

Wiley Publishing, Inc.

Published by:

WILEY PUBLISHING, INC.
111 River St.
Hoboken, NJ 07030-5774

ISBN-13: 978-0-470-04899-3
ISBN-10: 0-470-04899-9

Editor: Stephen Bassman
Production Editor: Eric T. Schroeder
Photo Editor: Richard Fox
Cartographer: Andrew Dolan
Anniversary Logo Design: Richard Pacifico
Production by Wiley Indianapolis Composition Services

For information on our other products and services or to obtain technical support, please contact our Customer Care Department within the U.S. at 800/762-2974, outside the U.S. at 317/572-3993 or fax 317/572-4002.

Wiley also publishes its books in a variety of electronic formats. Some content that appears in print may not be available in electronic formats.

Manufactured in the United States of America

5 4 3 2 1

Contents

3   Where to Stay in Providenciales & the Caicos Islands   60

4   Where to Dine on Providenciales & the Caicos Islands   82

5   Exploring Providenciales & the Caicos Islands   98

List of Maps

ABOUT THE AUTHOR

Alexis Lipsitz Flippin is a freelance writer and former Frommer's Senior Editor. She has written and edited for consumer magazines such as *Self, American Health,* and *Rolling Stone* and was an editor for *Reader's Digest* General Books.

ACKNOWLEDGMENTS

First of all, I'd like to thank my excellent guide, Nakier Wilson, of the Turks & Caicos Islands Tourist Board. I'd also like to thank the following individuals for their enormous help and support, in no particular order: Pamela Ewing, Turks & Caicos Tourist Board; Butch Clare, the Meridian Club; Nikheel Advani and Tina Lyra, the Grace Bay Club; Foluso Ladejob, the Palms; Patsy Thompson, Sibonne; Lucas Chanter, Point Grace; Andre Niederhauser, Coral Gardens; Joseph Zellner, Beaches; Pierre Beswick, The Sands of Grace Bay; Camille Slattery, Provo Ponies; Susie Gardiner, Pelican Beach Hotel; Alveda and Charlie, Hollywood Beach Suites; Cardinal Arthur, Middle Caicos; Lemano Malcolm, Grand Turk; Katrina Birt and Sandy Erb, Grand Turk Inn; Jenny Carnahan, the Osprey Beach Hotel; Colin Brooker, the Island House; Porter Williams, Island Thyme Bistro; Debbie Been, Salt Cay Divers; Pat Simmons, Pat's Place; and last but certainly not least, Nathan Smith, the unofficial mayor of Salt Cay.

AN INVITATION TO THE READER

In researching this book, we discovered many wonderful places—hotels, restaurants, shops, and more. We're sure you'll find others. Please tell us about them, so we can share the information with your fellow travelers in upcoming editions. If you were disappointed with a recommendation, we'd love to know that, too. Please write to:

Frommer's Portable Turks & Caicos, 1st Edition
Wiley Publishing, Inc. • 111 River St. • Hoboken, NJ 07030-5774

AN ADDITIONAL NOTE

Please be advised that travel information is subject to change at any time—and this is especially true of prices. We therefore suggest that you write or call ahead for confirmation when making your travel plans. The authors, editors, and publisher cannot be held responsible for the experiences of readers while traveling. Your safety is important to us, however, so we encourage you to stay alert and be aware of your surroundings. Keep a close eye on cameras, purses, and wallets, all favorite targets of thieves and pickpockets.

FROMMER'S STAR RATINGS, ICONS & ABBREVIATIONS

Every hotel, restaurant, and attraction listing in this guide has been ranked for quality, value, service, amenities, and special features using a **star-rating system.** In country, state, and regional guides, we also rate towns and regions to help you narrow down your choices and budget your time accordingly. Hotels and restaurants are rated on a scale of zero (recommended) to three stars (exceptional). Attractions, shopping, nightlife, towns, and regions are rated according to the following scale: zero stars (recommended), one star (highly recommended), two stars (very highly recommended), and three stars (must-see).

In addition to the star-rating system, we also use **seven feature icons.** that point you to the great deals, in-the-know advice, and unique experiences that separate travelers from tourists. Throughout the book, look for:

Finds	Special finds—those places only insiders know about
Fun Fact	Fun facts—details that make travelers more informed and their trips more fun
Kids	Best bets for kids and advice for the whole family
Moments	Special moments—those experiences that memories are made of
Overrated	Places or experiences not worth your time or money
Tips	Insider tips—great ways to save time and money
Value	Great values—where to get the best deals

The following **abbreviations** are used for credit cards:

AE	American Express	DISC	Discover	V	Visa
DC	Diners Club	MC	MasterCard		

FROMMERS.COM

Now that you have the guidebook to a great trip, visit our website at **www.frommers.com** for travel information on more than 3,500 destinations. With features updated regularly, we give you instant access to the most current trip-planning information available. At Frommers.com, you'll also find the best prices on airfares, accommodations, and car rentals—and you can even book travel online through our travel booking partners. At Frommers.com, you'll also find the following:

- Online updates to our most popular guidebooks
- Vacation sweepstakes and contest giveaways
- Newsletter highlighting the hottest travel trends
- Online travel message boards with featured travel discussions

The Best of the Turks & Caicos Islands

For years, the Turks & Caicos Islands' considerable natural attributes were known to just a fortunate few—many of them divers and snorkelers exploring the stunning ring of coral reefs and dramatic drop-offs of the continental shelf wall. But the sun-kissed archipelago is undiscovered no more: Overnight, it seems, resorts, restaurants, and tour operators have sprung up like mushrooms after a spring rain. Construction along the beauteous 19km (12 miles) of Grace Bay Beach is fashioning a lineup of sleek condos and resort hotels, and the tourist infrastructure is racing to catch up. Notoriously potholed dirt roads have been neatly paved (sidewalks even!), and a brand-new Hotel School at the Grace Bay Club is helping train a first-generation hospitality community.

Even with all the madcap development the islands have undergone in the last 5 years, the Turks & Caicos Islands (or "the TCI") have retained their getaway-vacation feel. The islands are best appreciated if you prefer your pleasures laid-back. If your idea of entertainment is 24-hour steel drums on the beach or a superheated nightlife, you may be disappointed (I take that back—there's always Club Med). The partying is more a sip-a-beer-in-a-beach-shack variety, with shade from casuarina trees and unencumbered views of that incredible turquoise sea.

This is not to say that you can't get your fill of high-adrenaline outdoor adventures. You can scuba-dive a vertical undersea wall where the continental shelf drops a heart-stopping mile deep (*Scuba Diving* magazine named the TCI one of the top 10 best diving sites in the world). You can parasail high over Grace Bay and actually swim alongside humpback whales or velvety stingrays. You can cast a line for bonefish, reef fish, night fish—or free-dive 6m (20 ft.) down to the sea bottom for fresh conch.

Still, what is most remarkable, in even the most heavily touristed spots like Grace Bay, is what you *don't* experience. You never hear the roar of jet skis or scores of motorboats (the coral reef is a protected national park and simply too shallow in spots to allow powerboats and personal water craft to be rented without a captain aboard in most cases). You don't see giant water parks rising up over the horizon or sunbathers packed cheek by jowl. You aren't confronted by an army of pushy hucksters roaming the beach.

And don't even bother coming if you're looking for a shopping spree. The island has one "mall," but chain retailers and superstores have yet to make inroads here—no Gap, no Target. You won't even see those mega T-shirt shops that have become ubiquitous in many seaside resorts. You *can* buy T-shirts, for sure, both of the generic tourist variety and more personalized versions, at boutique shops scattered about in the few retail clusters on the island. You can find good art by local artists in established galleries, but you also have the opportunity to seek out the source yourself, down an unpaved road, perhaps, with "potcake" dogs (island dogs traditionally fed from the bottom of the pot) licking your ankles and bougainvillea blossoms covering the ground.

In fact, you won't find a typical chain-*anything* here, so if you can't go 3 days without a fast-food burger, you may be a little grumpy after a week on the TCI. But you can get more-than-acceptable nonchain burgers, pizzas, and any kind of Western-style grub you desire—as well as some of the best food in the Caribbean. Expect to pay bruising big-city prices for anything you eat, however; it's tough to grow anything in this parched, sandy terrain, and most foodstuffs have to be imported.

Indeed, if you like your Caribbean islands thrillingly lush and mountainous, the dry scrubland terrain of the TCI may underwhelm you. But if you dream of lying on a pristine parcel of sugary sand encircled by a mesmerizing aquamarine sea, or want nothing more than to spend an afternoon happily bubbling about a living, breathing coral reef with mask and snorkel, book a trip now.

For a thumbnail portrait of each island, see "The Islands in Brief," in chapter 2.

1 The Best Beaches

Surrounded by the world's third-largest coral reef, the Turks & Caicos Islands have some of the finest powdery-sand beaches and most ethereal turquoise seas in the world. Most are just minutes away from an airport, and you'll rarely have to vie for beach space with anyone else. Tour boats can whisk you to uninhabited cays where you can play Robinson Crusoe for a day. The waters are pristine and diamond-clear, and waves rarely rise above a gentle ripple—perfect for young kids and snorkelers of all ages.

- **Grace Bay** (Providenciales): These 19km (12 miles) of pale sands and azure seas are the pride of Provo; *Condé Nast Traveler* has called this one of the world's best beaches. An increasing number of resorts and condo hotels have sprung up along the shore. Like much of the TCI, the beach is fringed by a coral reef system with fabulous snorkeling and diving. See chapter 5.
- **Malcolm Beach** (Providenciales): The traditional way to see this charming cove (often referred to as Malcolm Roads Beach) is with a 4×4 along twisting, bumpy Malcolm Roads. You can also access the beach by staying at Amanyara (the resort is adjacent to the beach) or by getting a tour-boat operator to take you there. Its waters are part of the Northwest Point Marine National Park. See chapter 5.
- **Long Bay** (Providenciales): The calm, shallow waters of this quiet beach on Provo's southeastern shore make it perfect for young children. Take a horseback ride on the beach here with Provo Ponies. See chapter 5.
- **Sapodilla Bay and Taylor Bay** (Providenciales): Part of the Chalk Sound National Park, these beautiful, shallow bays along Provo's southwest coastline have soft silty bottoms and warm water. See chapter 5.
- **Pine Cay** (Caicos Cays): The money shot in *Caribbean Travel & Life*'s coverage of the 2005–06 winter season? A pic of this private island's perfect crescent of pale white sand rimmed by azure seas. The island is also home to The Meridian Club. See chapters 3 and 5.
- **Parrot Cay** (Caicos Cays): Another gorgeous private island, this one with a secluded beach graced by beach bums of the celebrity variety. See chapter 3 and 5.
- **Sandy Point** (North Caicos): Up until now, only boaters and those in the know found their way to this crescent of perfect beach, within sight of the Parrot Cay Resort. Ground was broken in 2006 for construction of the Royal Reef Resort, a luxury hotel and condos fronting the beach. See chapters 3 and 5.
- **Whitby beaches** (North Caicos): The coves of Three Mary Cays are prime snorkeling spots. Step into the shallows of the palm-fringed Pelican Point beach (in front of Pelican Beach Hotel) and find conch shells of every size. Lovely Horsestable Beach has enjoyed its North Caicos seclusion for years (it's also

Best Beaches in the Turks & Caicos Islands

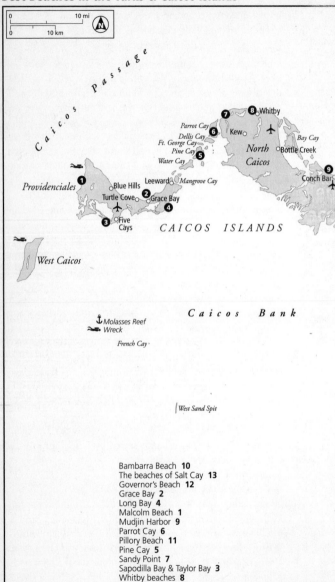

0   10 mi
0   10 km

Caicos Passage

Parrot Cay
Dellis Cay
Ft. George Cay
Pine Cay
Water Cay

Whitby **8**
7
Kew
6
Bay Cay
Bottle Creek
North Caicos

9
Conch Bar

Providenciales
1
Blue Hills
Turtle Cove
2
Grace Bay
Leeward
Mangrove Cay
4
3 Five Cays

CAICOS ISLANDS

West Caicos

Caicos Bank

Molasses Reef
Wreck

French Cay

West Sand Spit

ATLANTIC

OCEAN

10 Bambarra
Lorimers
Middle Caicos

East Caicos

South Caicos
Cockburn Harbour
Six Hill Cays
Long Cay

Fish Cay

Big Ambergris Cay
Little Ambergris Cay

Seal Cays *Bush Cay*

Turks Islands Passage

Grand Turk
Cockburn Town **11**
TURKS ISLANDS
Long Cay **12**
Cotton Cay
East Cay
Balfour Town *Salt Cay*
13

Mouchoir Passage

Big Sand Cay
⚓ *HMS Endymion Wreck*

a prime bird-watching spot); now it's the future home of the $70-million St. Charles condominium resort. See chapters 3 and 5.

- **Mudjin Harbor** (Middle Caicos): This beach is as stunning seen from the green limestone cliffs towering above as it is in an up-close exploration of the wind-swept coves below. See chapter 5.

- **Bambarra Beach** (Middle Caicos): Casuarina trees fringe this picturesque white-sand beach. Its calm, shallow aquamarine waters are the site of the festive Valentine's Day model sailboat races, and the Middle Caicos Day beach party is held here in August. See chapter 5.

- **Governor's Beach** (Grand Turk): Grand Turk's most celebrated beach has great snorkeling and is a popular picnic spot under shady pines. It's in the Columbus Landfall National Park—more about Columbus's "landfall" later—and within sightlines of the new Grand Turk Cruise Center, which in 2006 began welcoming 2,000-passenger ships 2 days a week. See chapter 6.

- **Pillory Beach** (Grand Turk): The Bohio Dive Resort is set on this handsome stretch of Grand Turk beach. See chapter 6.

- **The beaches of Salt Cay:** This tiny island has some of the best snorkeling beaches in the Caribbean. The calmest waters are usually found on North Beach and Point Pleasant. See chapter 6.

2 The Best Outdoor Adventures

The waters here are superlative for all kinds of outdoor adventures, from diving and snorkeling to sailing, kayaking, and fishing. But watersports aren't the only game in town. You'll find prime golf and tennis facilities in Provo—and Rollerblade hockey is all the rage with local school kids. See chapters 5 and 6 for more on outdoor sports.

- **Snorkeling the islands:** Stellar snorkeling opportunities are found throughout the islands, whether the Caicos Cays, North Caicos, Middle Caicos, South Caicos, Grand Turk, or Salt Cay (which some claim has the country's best snorkeling), but you can also snorkel right off Provo's spectacular Grace Bay Beach. The government has established snorkel trails at Smith's Reef and Bight Reef, right in front of the Reef Residences Coral Gardens resort (the hotel even has an on-site dive-and-snorkel instructor).

These reefs are right off the shoreline, providing easy access into a fragile but beautiful world. See chapter 5.

- **Taking a beachcombing cruise** (Caicos Cays): A number of tour-boat operators offer variations on half- and full-day beachcombing sojourns. Your trip may include a stop on **Little Water Cay,** a nature reserve set aside to protect the colony of rare rock iguanas; snorkeling the coral reefs and diving for conch; or combing the beaches of uninhabited cays for sand dollars and other shells. See "Caicos Water Sports Operators: Master List" box on p. 102.

- **Riding horses on the beach** (Long Bay, Provo): You don't need a whit of riding experience to thoroughly enjoy a leisurely late-afternoon trot on a beautiful beach. The gentle mounts of Provo Ponies are perfect for novices, but they don't mind kicking it up a bit for proven riders—they love the beach, too. See chapter 5.

- **Strolling Grace Bay before sunset:** You'll be surprised at the long stretches of beautiful beach you have all to yourself (and perhaps a few friendly "potcake" dogs). The sand is a little cooler, and the water takes on the pink and purple hues of the setting sun. Stop in and sink into an inviting white-cushioned perch at the **Lounge** (p. 67), the wonderful oceanfront bar at Grace Bay Club, and sip a cocktail while you wait for the green flash on the horizon. See chapter 5.

- **Watching the glowworms glow:** Four or 5 days after a full moon, millions of glowworms come out just after sunset to mate—lighting up the shallow local waters with a sparkling green glow. You can see them on a glowworm cruise in the Caicos Cays or off any number of Caicos Bank docks. The show is over after the females devour the males when the mating ritual ends. See chapter 5.

- **Hiking or biking the Crossing Place Trail** (Middle Caicos): This old coastal road, first established in the late 1700s by settlers working the local plantations, has been reopened from the Conch Bar to the Indian Cave field-road section and is now a National Trust heritage site. It has heartbreakingly beautiful sections, some on bluffs overlooking the blue-green ocean shallows and rocky outcrops; others bordered by island brush that includes wild sea-island cotton, remnants of the 18th-century plantations, and elegant sisal. Follow hiking or biking trails; when you get hot, take a swim in the shallow coves below. Be

sure to visit **Conch Bar Cave,** a massive aboveground limestone cave system that was used by Lucayan Indians some 600
years ago. See chapter 5.

- **Diving the Wall off Grand Turk:** You can find great scuba-
diving spots throughout the TCI, including spectacular opportunities off Provo's Northwest Point and in West Caicos. But
Grand Turk's electrifying dives are just some 274m (900 ft.)
offshore, where the continental shelf drops off from the coral
reef in dramatic fashion. Along the ledges of this sheer wall is
marine life in all its eye-popping plumage. See p. 133.

- **Whale-Watching on Salt Cay:** From January through April,
humpback whales migrate along the 7,000-foot trench of the
Columbus Passage (which runs between the Turks islands and
the Caicos islands) to the Silver Banks to mate and calf. You
can actually snorkel and swim alongside these 15m (50-ft.)
creatures. See chapter 6.

- **Finding treasures on the beach:** The currents drop off a good
amount of flotsam on these windward TCI beaches—much of
it worthless junk. But hey, one man's trash is another man's
treasure. Nearly every island has a visionary artist or two who
finds inspiration (and raw materials) in beach salvage. Of
course, you never know what will wash up: In 2006, silver
pieces of eight and an 18th-century spyglass were picked up on
the Salt Cay beaches. And bottles containing messages have
found their way here from all over the world; the Turks &
Caicos National Museum even has a collection of messages in
a bottle. The water's edge also yields gorgeous shells, from
snow white sand dollars to queen conch shells—but remember: Always return a shell back into the sea if it has something
living inside. (And shell collecting is not permitted in the
national parks.) See chapters 5 and 6.

3 Frommer's Favorite Luxury Resorts

Most of the country's accommodations are on Providenciales, where
more and more resort/condo hotels are being constructed as this is
written. The Northwest Point is a particularly hot area, with Amanresorts' much-anticipated Amanyara opening in 2006 and another
luxury resort in the works nearby.

- **Amanyara,** Northwest Point, Provo (© 866/941-8133): The
Singapore-based Amanresorts' first foray into the West Indies
is a hit, deftly marrying unparalleled pampered luxury with a

laidback Turks & Caicos aesthetic; the name means "peaceful place." The guest pavilions are huge, beautifully appointed in typical Aman teakwood, and completely private. See p. 76.

- **Parrot Cay Resort,** Parrot Cay, Provo (② 877/754-0726): Yes, this is the exclusive island resort where Ben Affleck married Jennifer Garner and Bruce Willis owns a home. But it's also a pretty wonderful place to completely unwind and de-stress, whether you're stretched out on the secluded beach or thrilling to a treatment by a Balinese masseuse at the world-class COMO Shambhala spa. See p. 78.

- **Grace Bay Club,** Grace Bay Road, Grace Bay (② 800/946-5757): One of the Grace Bay pioneers continues to upgrade and reinvent itself, and it just gets better and better. Everything, from the spacious luxury suites to the alfresco beachfront Lounge, is done just right. You can even have a staff chef cook you and your friends a gourmet dinner in your suite's state-of-the-art kitchen. See p. 66.

- **The Palms,** Grace Bay Road, Grace Bay (② 866/877-7256): There are no bad rooms at this voluptuous Miami-style resort, with gorgeous pools and restaurants and a 25,000-square-foot spa with reflecting pools. Try the mother-of-pearl-scrub spa treatment, which uses hand-crushed queen conch shells blended with aromatic oils. See p. 68.

- **The Meridian Club,** Pine Cay, Provo (② 866/746-3229): This is luxury of a different kind, where 12 comfortable suites—sans TV, phones, radios, even air-conditioning—on a secluded private island offer the kind of solitude and serenity found in few places in the world. The beach and watersports opportunities are superb. See p. 79.

- **Point Grace,** Grace Bay, Provo (② 866/924-7223): Set on a stunning bend on Grace Bay Beach, this resort gets consistent high marks for its spacious, handsomely furnished British colonial–style suites, lovely pool, and ultraromantic restaurant, Grace's Cottage, one of Provo's best places to dine. See p. 69.

- **Grand Turk Inn,** Front Street, Grand Turk (②/fax 649/946-2827): The big, comfortable suites are laid-back luxury personified. The innkeepers, sisters who've lived all over the world, are hospitality pros, and their loving restoration of the 150-year-old Methodist manse has created Grand Turk's best accommodations. See p. 127.

- **Windmills Plantation,** Salt Cay (② 649/946-6962): It's hard to put a label on a place so emblematic of its original owners'

Foluso Ladejobi's Favorite TCI Experiences

British-born Foluso Ladejobi vacationed on the Turks & Caicos Islands 20 years ago and never went home. Over the years she has been a schoolteacher and a resort planner and is now ensconced in the executive offices of The Palms resort—and her knowledge of TCI activities and entertainments is vast. Here are Foluso's favorite things to do on the islands:

- **Taking a sunset cruise on the catamaran** *Beluga* to the Caicos Cays with Captain Tim.
- **Seeing the glowworms light up the water** at Sapodilla Bay. The best place to see the glowworms is right at the dock. Go just before sunset, and take flashlights and coolers with drinks. We like to take driftwood, make a bonfire, and roast marshmallows.
- **Parasailing over Grace Bay.** You can go in threes—perfect for me and my two kids.
- **Drinking a cocktail at Amanyara** at sunset.
- **Indulging in a spa day at The Palms** with a mother-of-pearl scrub followed by a massage—definitely decadent.
- **Taking a beach excursion.** Have a tour-boat operator drop you off at a deserted beach for a beach barbecue or even catch fresh conch for you. I recommend J&B Tours, Catch the Wave Charters, Silver Deep, or Big Blue.
- **Visiting Grand Turk,** not only for the diving but to spend time in the Turks & Caicos National Museum. It's small and personal, but all of the islands' history is there in that old Bermudan building. I was also impressed with the colorful services at Grand Turk's Methodist Church; the choir is fantastic.
- **Dining at the Caicos Café,** especially on Friday nights when it's full of locals. I also love the food at the Sushi Bar, next to the Graceway IGA.

singular tastes and whims. But if you like your luxury lodgings with a distinctly boho flavor and more than a touch of whimsy, head here to tiny Salt Cay's only high-end resort. From afar, the otherworldly setting resembles some dusty island outpost out of *Alice in Wonderland,* the roofs of the inn's fanciful structures splashed in bright blues, reds, and yellows. See p. 142.

4 The Best Moderately Priced Lodgings

Let's face it: Bargain hotel rooms in Provo are increasingly few and far between (you can still find affordable lodging on the other islands, however). Keep in mind that one way to save on hotel rates is by taking advantage of the special packages advertised on most hotel websites, offering decreased rates and extra perks with extended stays. You can also find good hotel (and hotel/air) packages on popular travel-booking websites like Expedia and Travelocity, particularly in the off season (mid-Apr to Nov). And don't forget to look into villa rentals (see chapter 2 for more information). Here are my choices for the best of the islands' less-expensive accommodations.

- **Sibonné Beach Hotel,** Grace Bay, Provo (© **800/528-1905**): This place gives you a room only steps away from the waters of Grace Bay for a steal. Small and charming Sibonné is one of the oldest resorts on Grace Bay, and its rooms—all of which have sea views, by the way—are nothin' fancy but nicely appointed. But the real steal is the oceanfront apartment with full kitchen and two patios—one screened and one open, each with a meltingly lovely view of Grace Bay that many of the more chichi resorts would die for. See p. 75.

- **Caribbean Paradise Inn,** Grace Bay, Provo (© **877/946-5020**): The owner, Jean Luc Bohic, has a little gem of a B&B here, a 2-minute stroll from prime Grace Bay Beach. All rooms are set around the tropical courtyard and pool. Jean Luc is refreshing all the rooms, and he hopes to open a restaurant on the patio by late 2006. See p. 73.

- **Comfort Suites,** Grace Bay, Provo (© **888/678-3483**): This is a comfortable place to stay; the pool area is attractive, and the suites are spacious. And the location is prime: 1 block from Grace Bay and just across from the Ports of Call shops. See p. 74.

- **Pelican Beach Hotel,** Pelican Beach, North Caicos (© **649/946-7112**): The price is right at this small, comfortable spot smack dab on Pelican Point. Rooms are admittedly nothing special, but the beach is grand—and the food, cooked by owner Susie Gardiner, is superb home-style island fare. See p. 80.

- **Osprey Beach Hotel,** Duke Street, Grand Turk (© **649/946-2666**): You're in the thick of the Duke Street action, yet you're just steps away from the solitude of the island's southwestern beach. Many of the rooms have been newly refreshed with four-poster beds and cool white linens, and all are large and clean; those in the main section have private oceanfront patios. You'll see lots of familiar faces from all over the island at the Sunday night barbecue around the pool. See p. 128.

- **Island House,** Lighthouse Road, Grand Turk (© **649/946-1519**): The British-born owner, Colin Brooker, is charm personified, and his small inn perched on a Grand Turk hill has killer views of the sea and the island's gently sloping green bluffs. The freshwater pool lies in a lovely courtyard filled with tropical vegetation. You aren't on the beach, but Colin provides all his guests with a pickup truck to get around the island. See p. 128.

- **Bohio Dive Resort,** Front Street, Grand Turk (© **649/946-2135**): Set in a prime location on beautiful Pillory Beach, this hotel has big, clean rooms (the suites have kitchenettes) and offers reasonable dive/lodging packages. Its restaurant has one of the few true (read: classically trained) chefs on the island in Zev Beck. See p. 127.

5 Frommer's Favorite Dining Experiences

All the major islands offer diving trips, lessons, and equipment, but here are the top picks:

- **Anacaona,** Grace Bay Road, Provo (© **649/946-5050**): The setting for the Grace Bay Club's premier restaurant is unbeatable: You're seated under the stars, surrounded by flaming torches, on a tiered and lushly planted landing overlooking Grace Bay Beach. The food is up to the setting's challenge—especially anything prepared with fish. See p. 88.

- **Grace's Cottage,** Point Grace Hotel, Grace Bay (© **649/946-5096**): You'll see plenty of couples holding hands on these candlelit cottage patios (outdoors, amid gorgeous tropical vegetation)—but all hands quickly fall away when the grub arrives. The setting is lovely and charming indeed, but the food is superb. See p. 89.

- **Da Conch Shack,** Blue Hills, Provo (© **649/946-8877**): Formerly the hugely popular Bugaloos, now with new ownership and a location closer to downtown Provo, Da Conch Shack is one of those blessed spots that has it all: great setting (outdoors on a Blue Hills beach), killer fresh food (conch pulled out of its shell on the beach below and prepared to order), and a joyful, laid-back, barefoot vibe. See p. 84.

- **Caicos Café,** Caicos Café Plaza, Grace Bay Road, Provo (© **649/946-5278**): This is a popular spot among the locals, and it's easy to see why: The place couldn't be more convivial. Set on a spacious Caribbean-style wooden deck, the restaurant is all lit up for dinner with torches and strings of twinkling lights, and the fanciful gingerbread woodwork and island art covering the walls add to the ambience. The cuisine is French-Caribbean, and the shrimp risotto is a popular choice. See p. 91.
- **Magnolia Wine Bar & Restaurant,** Turtle Cove, Provo (© **649/941-5108**): The view alone is worth the trek up the hill above Turtle Cove marina, but the food easily stands on its own. Seared rare tuna is a house specialty. See p. 96.
- **Baci Ristorante,** Turtle Cove, Harbour Towne, Provo (© **649/941-3044**): This Italian restaurant has a great setting, right on the docks of the Turtle Cove marina. Lacy iron doors lead out to terraced outdoor seating on the water. The food is standard Italian—fettuccine Alfredo, lasagne alla Bolognese—but hearty and good, and a refreshing break from all that conch. See p. 95.
- **Hemingway's on the Beach,** The Sands at Grace Bay, Provo (© **649/941-8408**): With a location this good (right on Grace Bay Beach, at The Sands on Grace Bay resort), this spot doesn't have to be this dependable. But it's packed day and night, largely because the food is consistently tasty and fresh. Everyone serves conch chowder, but few are as good as Hemingway's. And don't get me started on the coconut shrimp. See p. 93.
- **Pat's Place,** Historic South District, Salt Cay (© **649/946-6919**): Pat taught school on Salt Cay for 28 years. She now serves tasty home-style island cooking on a modest porch behind her home. You'll feel like Mom is behind the stove when she brings out her family-style platters of barbecued chicken, potato salad, and rice and peas. See p. 143.

2

Planning Your Trip to the Turks & Caicos Islands

This chapter tackles the how-tos of a trip to the TCI, everything from finding airfares to deciding whether to rent a car. But first, let's start with some background information about this increasingly popular destination.

1 Getting to Know Turks & Caicos

It seems only yesterday that public awareness of this island archipelago was essentially "Turks & Caicos who?" For years, these islands were little more than a beautiful, slumbering backwater, home to a close-knit society of islanders called "Belongers," and the haunt of a smattering of fishermen and divers, beach bums and drug smugglers, and, of course, the well-heeled looking for an untouched cay in which to drop anchor.

Today the TCI is fast on its way to becoming one of the premier destinations in the Caribbean, winning numerous travel industry accolades—including the 2005 World Travel Awards for World's Leading Beach (Grace Bay) and World's Leading Boutique Hotel (Point Grace). Air flights were up 25% in the year 2005 alone. So far, the tourist boom has been largely concentrated on the main island, Providenciales ("Provo" for short). While many of the outlying islands retain the feel of an idyllic outpost that time has forgotten, Provo is the fastest-growing spot in the Caribbean, its dazzling beaches attracting upscale hotels and boutique resorts—including Amanresorts' first foray into the West Indies, Amanyara, in 2006.

Still, Provo isn't the only Turks & Caicos (pronounced *Kayk*-us) island romancing the tourist dollar. Sleepy Grand Turk is getting something of a wake-up call, with a projected quarter-million cruise-ship passengers scheduled to disembark at the spiffy new cruise terminal in 2006. The Ritz-Carlton is developing a high-end, low-impact hotel/condo/resort/village in the heretofore uninhabited West Caicos, a national reserve. And amid the little fishing villages

A Little History

The earliest inhabitants of these islands were Lucayan Indians, who settled in the Bahamas archipelago some 800 years before Columbus arrived in the New World. Some historians believe that Grand Turk was the site of Columbus's first landfall—and experts have established that the explorer was indeed greeted on his arrival by Lucayan Indians—but no hard evidence exists to support this theory either way. The Lucayans' idyllic existence came to an end when Spanish explorers arrived, enslaving the natives and exposing them to diseases. In a generation, the Lucayan population was wiped out. Habitation was spotty after that, with the islands passing through Spanish, French, and British control and industries coming and going—from **salt-raking,** which drew Bermudans—and the British crown—in the late 17th century, to **cotton,** which brought Loyalists fleeing the States after the American Revolution. The cotton industry was eventually done in by storms and pests, and by the early 19th century, the main inhabitants left on the islands were the slaves that had been brought in to work the plantations. The salt industry—labor-intensive work that broke the backs of many a worker in the tropical heat—lasted until the 1960s, around the time a small airstrip was built on Provo and a nascent tourist industry began to stir. But it wasn't until 1984, when the development of Club Med led to the construction of a larger airport, that commercial tourism started to take root on the Turks & Caicos Islands.

of South Caicos, the island of Ambergris Cay is being transformed into the Turks & Caicos Sporting Club by the renowned Greenbrier Resort.

Why is little TCI ripe for all this activity? For one, the country's beaches, water, and coral reef system remain astonishingly unspoiled. The seas have an intense blue-green hue that puts Technicolor to shame. The climate—best described as an "eternal summer"—is ideal year-round. Gentle breezes blowing in from the east provide relief from the relentless sun. For North Americans, the TCI has other pluses: English is the official language, the U.S. dollar is the local currency, and the islands are incredibly accessible by plane: Nonstop flights out of places like New York City (3 hr.), Boston (3½ hr.), Charlotte (2 hr.), and Miami (1½ hr.) mean you can jump on a plane in the morning and be lazing about on a tropical beach by early afternoon.

The islands also enjoy zero unemployment—and, probably not unrelated—the lowest crime rate in the Caribbean; you simply do not see the kind of impoverishment and homelessness that continue to plague other Caribbean countries. The TCI government is stable (the TCI is a British protectorate with a representative democracy and a constitution), and the island citizens—"the Belongers"— enjoy one of the best primary and secondary educational systems in the region. The Belongers share such a warm familiarity that it's easy to see why many have embraced the possibility that all are connected by blood, descended from the 193 African slaves freed on these isolated islands when the slave ship *Trouvadore,* carrying them to lives of bondage in the Americas, wrecked on the East Caicos reef in 1841. Research is underway by a Turks & Caicos National Museum expedition team to discern whether a shipwreck found off East Caicos in 2004 is the *Trouvadore*—and if so, whether its inhabitants were indeed the progenitors of the modern-day Belongers. For the latest information, go to www.slaveshiptrouvadore.com.

For those who knew and loved the TCI in slower times and who may be concerned that the islands are in danger of being overdeveloped (or even ruinously developed), it's comforting to know that of the 40 islands that comprise the TCI, only eight are inhabited. Even the most populous beach, Provo's Grace Bay, has long, dreamy stretches where you're the only soul on the soft sand. And except for a couple of scary concrete behemoths rising up out of the beach on Grace Bay (when did the oceanfront height limits jump from 5 stories to 10?), the focus has been on "sustainable development" and low-impact, high-end properties—boutique resorts with ecologically sensitive bones. Let's hope this vision holds through the fizzy boom times. In the meantime, TCI offers a fresh and exciting experience for travelers in search of a pristine (and accessible) island paradise.

2 The Islands in Brief

The TCI topography is pretty prosaic—all the islands are low lying, with sandy soil and a low scrub cover—but each island has its own unique look and feel. North Caicos, the so-called "garden island,"

Turks & Caicos at a Glance

Location: The Turks & Caicos archipelago is located in the British West Indies, 48km (30 miles) south of the Bahamas, 161km (100 miles) northeast of the Dominican Republic, and 925km (575 miles) southeast of Miami. The TCI is not officially in the Caribbean—it's in the Atlantic Ocean.

Population: The country's population is approximately 30,000 people. Citizens of the TCI, called "Belongers," are the descendants of African slaves and comprise more than half the islands' population. A large group of Haitian expats live and work in the TCI, but in 2006 the government stopped granting work permits to new Haitian arrivals. Other expat groups include a growing number of Filipinos.

Size: The two island groups—the Turks islands and the Caicos islands—together comprise 500 sq. km (193 sq. miles) and are separated by the 35km (22-mile) **Columbus Passage,** the sea route Christopher Columbus took during his exploration of the New World in 1492.

Economy: Tourism, fishing, and the offshore finance industry are the big three. Regarding the latter, the islands are a "zero tax" jurisdiction and have no taxes on income, capital gains, corporate profits, inheritance, or estates. There are no controls on transferring funds or assets in or out of the country.

Government: The TCI is a British Crown Colony. A queen-appointed governor holds executive power and presides over an Executive Council. A 1987 constitution established a representative democracy, and today the local government is elected by the citizens and includes a chief minister, other ministers, and a legislative council empowered to enact local statutes. The TCI seat of government is Cockburn Town in Grand Turk. The constitution was in the process of being modernized at press time, and rumblings of independence from Great Britain continue to make the news, especially at election time.

Last time the queen visited: 1968. She stopped in at South Caicos.

has a rural landscape rimmed by blue-green seas. Middle Caicos has soft emerald cliffs overlooking rocky coves, beaches fringed by casuarina trees, and the occasional cotton or sisal plant left over from plantation days. Grand Turk, Salt Cay, and South Caicos are low-key charmers that hold vivid architectural remnants of the islands' colonial past, while much in Provo (Providenciales) is as bright and shiny as a new penny. All have stupendously lovely soft-sand beaches lapped by pellucid azure seas.

In an interesting twist, the boom that hit Provo has drawn people to tourist-industry jobs away from their homes—and traditional livelihoods—on the other islands. In Middle Caicos in particular, you'll see homes abandoned to the underbrush and once-thriving communities reduced nearly to ghost towns. To ensure that the traditional cultures and way of life on the islands aren't lost forever, the **Turks & Caicos National Trust** has made it its mission to "safeguard the natural, historical and cultural heritage of the Turks & Caicos Islands." To find out more about the National Trust's latest projects, go to the website www.nationaltrust.tc.

THE CAICOS ISLANDS

Providenciales The gorgeous 19km (12-mile) beach and pristine coastline of 98-sq.-km (38-sq.-mile) **Providenciales (Provo)** were a tourist development waiting to happen. In the early 1980s, hotel megaliths such as Club Med poured money into increasingly popular low-rise eco-conscious resorts. Now Provo's tourist infrastructure far surpasses anything on Grand Turk, the TCI seat of government. This is where the action is, literally, with the bulk of the country's lodging, dining, tours, activities, and entertainment. Still, don't expect a bustling metropolis: Provo remains much sleepier than most other Caribbean islands—and that's a big part of its charm. One of the larger islands of the Turks and Caicos, Provo is green but arid, with miles of scrubland covering the island's low, undulating hills. Provo is the main destination for most people visiting the TCI.

Caicos Cays Also called the Leeward Cays, these gorgeous little islands were once the haven of pirates. Many are now uninhabited except by day-trippers beachcombing and snorkeling the shallows, while others are private islands with secluded resorts. Little Water Cay is a National Trust nature reserve that is home to the endangered rock iguana.

North Caicos The projected site of the second big TCI boom (they're breaking ground as we go to print) still has a sleepy rural landscape. Roads are dusty and potholed, beaches lovely and untrammeled, lodgings and restaurants admittedly few and far between. Locals say this sparsely populated, 106-sq.-km (41-sq.-mile) island is what Provo looked like before the boom.

Middle Caicos Middle Caicos is the largest island in the Turks & Caicos (125 sq. km/48 sq. miles), and has a remarkably varied landscape. Soft green slopes overlook beautiful Mudjin Harbor. Along the rise is Crossing Place Trail, a narrow 18th-century path so named because it leads to a place where people once crossed a sandbar at low tide to reach North Caicos. A massive aboveground limestone cave system was used by Lucayan Indians some 600 years ago. At Bambarra Beach the sunlit aquamarine waters stretch long into the horizon.

South Caicos This still-sleepy fishing community of some 1,200 people and 21 sq. km (8 sq. miles) is hearing faint rumblings of tourist development. Because the South Caicos tourist infrastructure is still in its infancy, this guide addresses the region only peripherally. But clearly, with its excellent diving and bonefishing opportunities and historic Bermudan-style architecture, "Big South" is an up-and-coming spot.

East Caicos This unspoiled, largely uninhabited 47-sq.-km (18-sq.-mile) island was once used for large sisal and cotton plantations. Now it's largely swampland and savanna.

West Caicos This lovely uninhabited 29-sq.-km (11-sq.-mile) island (with a 202-hectare/500-acre nature preserve) will be the home of a new five-star Ritz-Carlton resort (scheduled to open in 2008), with a 100-slip marina, villas, town houses, cottages, private homes, and the Molasses Reef Hotel. West Caicos is the site of the some of the islands' best scuba diving.

THE TURKS ISLANDS

Grand Turk People who only visit Provo miss out on experiencing the country's rich heritage. On the enchanting island of Grand Turk, just 11km by 3km (7×2 miles), these include a 150-year-old lighthouse, colorful 19th-century Bermudian architecture, abandoned salinas where the business of salt-raking was conducted from the late 17th century until the 1960s, and a first-rate museum housed in the Guinep House, believed to be around 180 years old. The laid-back, small-town atmosphere of Cockburn Town belies the fact that this Grand Turk village is the capital of the TCI. The diving here along the continental shelf wall is stupendous, the main draw for most visitors. That is, until 2006, when Carnival Cruise Lines opened a

The Turks & Caicos Islands

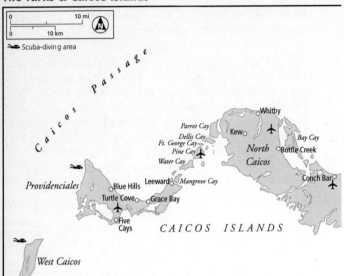

Scuba-diving area

Caicos Passage

Whitby

Parrot Cay
Dellis Cay
Ft. George Cay
Pine Cay
Water Cay

Kew

Bay Cay

North
Caicos

Bottle Creek

Conch Bar

Leeward
Mangrove Cay

Providenciales

Blue Hills
Turtle Cove
Grace Bay
Five Cays

CAICOS ISLANDS

West Caicos

Caicos Bank

Molasses Reef
Wreck
French Cay

West Sand Spit

ATLANTIC

OCEAN

theme-park-style cruise terminal at the southwest end of the island to welcome the arrival of 2,000 passenger ships. Still, Grand Turk's tourist infrastructure remains relatively undeveloped, with just a scattering of inns and hotels. The island is also home to feral donkeys and horses, the latter reputedly descended from Spanish mustangs shipwrecked here in the 16th century. Among the uninhabited cays in the Grand Turk Cays Land and Sea National Park is Gibbs Cay, where you can swim in the shallow water with stingrays.

Salt Cay   Salt Cay (population: 60) is the kind of place where you can paste salvaged flip-flops onto your neighbor's boat while he's away, and everyone (including your neighbor) thinks it's a hoot. It's the kind of place where a hermit crab race is the talk of the town. It's also the kind of place where people come from around the world to partake in world-class watersports activities (snorkeling, diving, whale-watching), swim in the luminescent green sea, and comb the secluded beaches for flotsam and jetsam. Salt Cay is admittedly small (6.5 sq. km/2½ sq. miles) and missing many of the basic accouterments of 21st-century civilization (no ATMs, just a handful of cars), but it is a place of haunting beauty and enormous heart.

3 Visitor Information

The **Turks & Caicos Tourist Board** (www.turksandcaicos tourism.com) has offices in Providenciales (Stubbs Diamond Plaza; ⓒ **649/946-4970**), Grand Turk (Front St., Cockburn Town; ⓒ **649/ 946-2321**), and New York City (Room 2817, the Lincoln Building, 60 E. 42nd St.; ⓒ **800/241-0824**). Office hours are Monday to Friday 8:30am to 4:30pm.

SIGHTSEEING ON THE WEB   The Internet is a great source of current travel information. "Planning Your Trip Online," later in this chapter, is a detailed guide that will help you use the Web to its best advantage to research and perhaps even book your trip.

Whenever possible throughout this book, we've included Web addresses along with phone numbers and addresses for attractions, outfitters, and other companies. We've also given each hotel and resort's website, so you can see pictures of a property before you make your reservation.

The following recommended Turks & Caicos–specific websites can be of enormous help in planning your trip.

- **www.provo.net**: Offers solid, up-to-date information on travel planning.

Tips **Calling Home**

Making international calls from the Turks & Caicos can be costly, in particular if you're dialing direct from your hotel room, where you are charged more than $2 a minute. You cannot access most U.S. toll-free numbers from the TCI; for example, you won't be able to use AT&T prepaid calling cards here. You can use any GSM cellphone if it has international roaming capabilities. One way to avoid the high costs of calling home from your hotel room is to **buy a prepaid cellphone** in the TCI. You can purchase a cellphone for as low as $60; it comes with a $10 phonecard. Additional prepaid phone cards come in $10, $20, $50, and $75 denominations. Phones and cards can be found at the **Cable & Wireless** offices on Leeward Highway (✆ **649/946-2200**) and at the Graceway IGA Supermarket (Cable & Wireless has a small office at the entrance). Another option is to **rent a cellphone. TCIonline Internet Café** (in the Ports of Call shopping center, Provo; ✆ **649/941-4711**) offers cellphone rentals ($150 deposit; $10/day; $50/week; phone time is charged to your credit card as you use minutes), as do Grant's Texaco Downtown and Kathleen's 7-Eleven on Leeward Highway.

- **www.turksandcaicos.tc**: This site, sponsored by Cable & Wireless, has an exhaustive amount of information. It's best in providing hardworking travel information and links on the less-traveled islands.
- **www.tcmuseum.org**: The Turks & Caicos National Museum is a delight, one of the best museums in the Caribbean, and this website is a wonderful reflection of the museum's collection, the islands' history and culture, and the ongoing research projects affiliated with the museum.
- **www.nationaltrust.tc**: The site of the Turks & Caicos National Trust, a nonprofit, nongovernmental organization dedicated to the preservation of the cultural, historical, and natural heritage of the Turks & Caicos Islands.
- **www.timespub.tc**: The website for the *Times of the Islands,* a quarterly magazine that has meaty features on TCI flora and fauna, history, culture, food, and business.

4 Entry Requirements & Customs

ENTRY REQUIREMENTS
PASSPORTS
U.S. and Canadian citizens must have a passport or a combination of a birth certificate and photo ID, plus a return or ongoing ticket, to enter the country. Citizens of the United Kingdom, Commonwealth countries of the Caribbean, the Republic of Ireland, and E.U. countries must also have a current passport.

All travelers coming from the Caribbean, including Americans, are now required to have a passport to enter or re-enter the United States. Those returning to Canada will have to show passports starting December 31, 2006. You'll certainly need identification at some point, and a passport is the best form of ID for speeding through Customs and Immigration. Driver's licenses are not acceptable as a sole form of ID.

CUSTOMS
Generally, you're permitted to bring in items intended for your personal use, including tobacco, cameras, film, and a limited supply of liquor—usually 40 ounces.

Just before you leave home, check with the Turks & Caicos Customs or Foreign Affairs department for the latest guidelines—including information on items that are not allowed to be brought into your home country—since the rules are subject to change and often contain some surprising oddities.

On arriving in the Turks & Caicos, you may bring in 1 quart of liquor, 200 cigarettes, 50 cigars, or 8 ounces of tobacco duty-free. There are no restrictions on cameras, film, sports equipment, or personal items, provided they aren't for resale. Absolutely no spear guns or Hawaiian slings are allowed, and the importation of firearms without a permit is also prohibited. Illegal imported drugs bring heavy fines and lengthy terms of imprisonment.

You should collect receipts for all purchases made abroad. You must also declare on your Customs form the nature and value of all gifts received during your stay abroad. It's prudent to carry proof that you purchased expensive cameras or jewelry on the U.S. mainland. If you purchased such an item during an earlier trip abroad, you should carry proof that you have previously paid Customs duty on the item.

Sometimes merchants suggest a false receipt to undervalue your purchase. *Beware:* You could be involved in a sting operation—the merchant might be an informer to U.S. Customs.

If you use any medication that contains controlled substances or requires injection, carry an original prescription or note from your doctor.

For specifics on what you can bring back, download the invaluable free pamphlet *Know Before You Go!* online at **www.cbp.gov**. (Click on "Travel," then click on "Know Before You Go.") Or contact the **U.S. Customs & Border Protection (CBP),** 1300 Pennsylvania Ave. NW, Washington, DC 20229 (© **877/287-8667**), and request the pamphlet.

U.K. citizens should contact **HM Customs & Excise** at © **0845/010-9000** (© 020/8929-0152 from outside the U.K.), or consult its website at www.hmce.gov.uk.

For a clear summary of **Canadian** rules, write for the booklet *I Declare,* issued by the **Canada Border Services Agency** (© **800/461-9999** in Canada, or 204/983-3500; www.cbsa-asfc.gc.ca).

Citizens of **Australia** should request a helpful brochure available from Australian consulates or Customs offices called *Know Before You Go.* For more information, call the **Australian Customs Service** at © **1300/363-263**, or log on to www.customs.gov.au.

For **New Zealand** Customs information, contact **New Zealand Customs** at © **04/473-6099** or 0800/428-786, or log on to www.customs.govt.nz.

5 Money

CASH/CURRENCY The U.S. dollar is the legal currency of the Turks & Caicos. Traveler's checks are accepted at most places, as are Visa, MasterCard, and American Express.

ATMs/ABMs The easiest and best way to get cash away from home is from an ATM. The **Cirrus** (© **800/424-7787**; www.mastercard.com) and **PLUS** (© **800/843-7587**; www.visa.com) networks span the globe; look at the back of your bank card to see which network you're on. The two banks with branches in the Turks

---

Tips Small Bills & Loose Change

It's a good idea to bring plenty of petty cash (small bills and loose change) for snacks, incidentals, and gratuities. There is no ATM at the Provo airport (or any airport for that matter). In fact, you'll find that **ATMs are few and far between on these islands.**

& Caicos are First Caribbean International Bank (PLUS network) and Scotiabank (Cirrus network)—but don't expect to find an ATM on every corner here. Other than the 24-hour ATMs at each bank's main location in Providenciales and Grand Turk, Scotiabank has two ATMs in Provo. For information on locations and opening times of First Caribbean and Scotiabank ATMs (also referred to as ABMs here), go to "Fast Facts: The Turks & Caicos Islands," at the end of this chapter.

Be sure you know your personal identification number (PIN) and your daily withdrawal limit before you leave home. Also keep in mind that many banks impose a fee every time a card is used at a different bank's ATM, and that fee can be higher for international transactions than for domestic ones. On top of this, the bank from which you withdraw cash may charge its own fee. For international withdrawal fees, ask your bank before you leave home.

TRAVELER'S CHECKS You can get traveler's checks at almost any bank. They are offered in denominations of $20, $50, $100, $500, and sometimes $1,000. Generally, you'll pay a service charge ranging from 1% to 4%.

The most popular traveler's checks are offered by American Express (© **800/807-6233** or 800/221-7282 for cardholders—this number accepts collect calls, offers service in several foreign languages, and exempts Amex gold and platinum cardholders from the 1% fee); **Visa** (© **800/732-1322**)—AAA members can obtain Visa checks for a $9.95 fee (for checks up to $1,500) at most AAA offices or by calling © **866/339-3378**; and **MasterCard** (© **800/223-9920**).

If you carry traveler's checks, be sure to keep a record of their serial numbers separate from your checks in the event that they are stolen or lost. You'll get a refund faster if you know the numbers.

CREDIT CARDS Credit cards are a safe way to carry money, they provide a convenient record of all your expenses, and they generally offer relatively good exchange rates. You can also withdraw cash advances from your credit cards at banks or ATMs, provided you know your PIN. Keep in mind that you'll pay interest from the moment of your withdrawal, even if you pay your monthly bills on time. Also note that many banks now assess a 1% to 3% "transaction fee" on all charges you incur abroad (whether you're using the local currency or your native currency).

Almost every credit card company has an emergency toll-free number that you can call if your wallet or purse is stolen. Credit card companies may be able to wire cash advances immediately, and in many places they can deliver an emergency credit card in a day or two. **Citicorp Visa**'s U.S. emergency number is ✆ **800/336-8472.** **American Express** cardholders and traveler's check holders should call ✆ **800/221-7282** for all money emergencies. **MasterCard** holders should call ✆ **800/307-7309.**

6 When to Go

THE WEATHER

The average temperature on the Turks & Caicos Islands ranges between 85°F and 90°F (29°C–32°C) from June to October, sometimes reaching the mid-90s (35°C), especially in the late summer months. From November to May the average temperature is 80°F to 84°F (27°C–29°C).

Water temperature in the summer is 82°F to 84°F (28°C–29°C) and in winter about 74°F to 78°F (23°C–26°C). A constant easterly trade wind keeps the climate at a very comfortable level.

Grand Turk and South Caicos have an annual rainfall of 53 centimeters (21 in.), but as you travel farther west, the average rainfall can increase to as much as 102 centimeters (40 in.). In an average year the Turks & Caicos Islands have 350 days of sunshine.

Mosquitoes and no-see-ums can be a problem year-round. However, more mosquitoes come out during the rainy season, which usually occurs in autumn.

If you come in the summer, be prepared for really broiling sun in the midafternoon.

If you want to know how to pack just before you go, check the Weather Channel's online 10-day forecast at **www.weather.com** for the latest information.

Average Temperatures (°F) and Rainfall

	Jan	Feb	Mar	Apr	May	Jun	Jul	Aug	Sep	Oct	Nov	Dec
Max (°F)	82	82	84	86	88	90	90	91	88	88	86	86
Max (°C)	28	28	29	30	31	32	32	33	31	31	30	30
Min (°F)	70	70	72	73	77	79	79	82	81	77	75	72
Min (°C)	21	21	22	23	25	26	26	28	27	25	24	22
Ave. rain (in.)	2	1.4	1.1	1.4	2.5	1.7	1.7	2	3.2	3.9	4.0	2.8

Source: Hutchinson World Weather Guide

HURRICANES   The curse of Caribbean weather, the hurricane season lasts—officially, at least—from June 1 to November 30. But there's no cause for panic: Satellite forecasts give enough warning that precautions can be taken.

The Turks & Caicos have been spared serious hurricane havoc in recent years; some say the mountains of Haiti and the Dominican Republic weaken hurricane-force winds before the storms reach the TCI. Still, hurricanes have wreaked havoc here in the past, including a September 1926 storm that brought 150-mph winds, slammed boulders on beaches, and had a storm surge that moved 1.2km (¾ miles) inland. In 1960 Hurricane Donna dropped 51 centimeters (20 in.) of rain in 24 hours. So it has happened—and no doubt will happen again. Always monitor weather reports if you plan to visit during hurricane season. Check the **Weather Channel** on the Web at **www.weather.com**.

THE HIGH SEASON & THE OFF SEASON

Like much of the Caribbean, the Turks & Caicos have become a year-round destination. The "season" runs roughly from mid-December to mid-April, which is generally the driest time of year in the Caribbean and the most miserable time of year in the U.S. Northeast and Midwest and in Canada. Hotels charge their highest prices during the peak winter period, and you'll have to make your reservations well in advance—months in advance if you want to travel over the Christmas or New Year's holidays or in the depths of February, especially around Presidents' Day weekend. The Easter holidays/school spring break is an increasingly popular time for families to visit.

The off season in the Turks & Caicos—roughly from mid-April to mid-November (although this varies from hotel to hotel)—is a perfectly nice time to come to the TCI: Yes, the temperatures are somewhat higher, but the southeasterly trade winds work to temper the heat, as do the brief but more frequent rain showers. The off season is also one big sale. In most cases, hotels, inns, and condos slash 20% to 50% off their winter rates. Airfares are generally cheaper, and air/hotel packages can be very reasonable—even for stays at the top luxury lodgings. But because the TCI has become so accessible from many North American cities, it's becoming more and more popular as an off-season destination. For many Europeans, who generally have longer vacation times, the summer is already a favorite time to visit the TCI.

Note: Some hotels use the off season for refurbishment or bustling construction projects—which can prove to be an annoyance if you're looking for peace and quiet. Make sure to ask what, if any, work is going on. If you decide to go anyway, ask for a room far away from the noise.

HOLIDAYS

New Year's Day (Jan 1); Commonwealth Day (observed on the Mon nearest Mar 12); Good Friday (celebrated the Fri prior to Easter); Easter Monday (celebrated on the Mon after Easter); National Heroes Day (observed the last Mon in May in honor of the First Chief Minister, the late Hon J.A.G.S. McCartney); Queen's Official Birthday (observed mid-June); Emancipation Day (celebrated the first of Aug; this holiday commemorates the freedom of the slaves, which was declared from Oddfellows Lodge in Grand Turk in 1834); National Youth Day (celebrated the last Fri of Sept); Columbus Day (celebrated on the Mon nearest Oct 10; this holiday commemorates Christopher Columbus' "landing" on TCI in 1492—although no firm evidence exists to confirm that the explorer actually made a landfall here at all); International Human Rights Day (observed on Oct 24; this holiday is similar to the USA's July Fourth celebration); Christmas Day (Dec 25); Boxing Day (Dec 26; on this day the annual Church Fair takes place in the Grand Turk Methodist Church).

TURKS & CAICOS CALENDAR OF EVENTS

January

Junkanoo, island-wide. Junkanoo is held throughout the year for public holidays and local events, but the biggest Junkanoo celebrations are on Emancipation Day, Boxing Day, and the early morning of New Year's Day. Groups compete against each other for the most outrageous costumes, the best drummers, the best rhythm section, and more. Midnight to sunrise, New Year's Day morning.

February

Valentine's Day Cup, Bambarra Beach, Middle Caicos. Traditional Model Sailboat Race, with trophies and other prizes, is followed by music, food, a domino tournament, and other festivities on the beach. The model sailboats are built in Bambarra from branches of the gum-elemi tree, constructed to scale with the actual rigging found on a full-size sloop. For more information, contact ✆ **649/941-7639** or **middlecaicos@tciway.tc**. Saturday closest to Valentine's Day.

March

St. Patrick's Day Pub Crawl, Providenciales. Contact © **649/ 946-2801.** March 17.

April

Carifta Games 2007, Providenciales. The 36th annual regional track-and-field Carifta Games are being hosted for the first time by the Turks & Caicos in their new National Stadium in 2007. Some 600 athletes from 26 countries in the English/French Caribbean will be in attendance for these events. Go to **www. carifta2007.tc**. April 6 and April 7.

Turks & Caicos Tourist Board 15th Annual Kite Flying Competition, Providenciales. Held in the Children's Park, on Lower Bight Road, this competition also features an Easter egg hunt, music, and a barbecue. Registration forms are available at the tourist board office in Provo. Call © **649/946-4970.** April 9.

May

Big South Regatta, South Caicos. The Big South Regatta, now in its 40th year, features boat races, concerts, food, and entertainers. Visit **www.bigsouthregatta.tc**. May 25 through May 29.

June

The Famous Fools Regatta, Providenciales. This beach party celebrating all things maritime features native sloops in sailing races, a sand-castle competition, and more. The regatta is held to raise funds for the Turks & Caicos Maritime Heritage Foundation for maritime educational projects for kids. Held at the Children's Park in the Bight. June 17.

Heineken Game Fishing Tournament, Grand Turk. Fish tourney at Governor's Beach features big cash prizes, music, barbecue, volleyball, and, of course, dominoes. For more information, call the Turks & Caicos Tourist Board at © **649/946-2321.** June 23 through June 25.

July

Loíza Carnival. This annual folk and religious ceremony honors Loíza's patron saint, John (Santiago) the Apostle. Colorful processions take place, with costumes, masks, and *bomba* dancers (the *bomba* has a lively Afro-Caribbean dance rhythm). This jubilant celebration reflects the African and Spanish heritage of the region. For more information, call © **787/886-6071.** Late July through early August.

Turks & Caicos Music & Cultural Festival (Providenciales). This 8-day affair is only in its third year, but it's already become a big deal, attracting big-name talent; the 2006 festival featured Ludacris and Fantasia, among other musicians, and performances were aired on BET. It also features pageants, parades, and regattas. For more information, go to **www.musicfestival.tc** or call ✆ **649/946-2321.** July 31 through August 7.

August

Emancipation Day, island-wide. Celebrating the freeing of the slaves, declared from Oddfellows Lodge in Grand Turk in 1834. First of August.

Middle Caicos Day, Middle Caicos. Parades, beauty pageants, music, food, and an all-day beach party at Bambarra Beach. For more information, contact ✆ **649/941-7639** or **middlecaicos@ tciway.tc**. Last weekend in August.

September

National Youth Day, island-wide. This public holiday celebrates the youth of the island. September 29.

October

TCI Amateur Open, Providenciales. Pricewaterhouse Coopers Limited sponsors this 3-day 36-hole championship for both men and women, now in its 12th year, at the Provo Golf & Country Club. For more information, go to **www.provogolfclub.com**. October 7, 8, and 9.

Columbus Day, island-wide. This public holiday celebrates Columbus's "discovery" of the New World. Legend has it that the explorer first came ashore at Grand Turk. October 9.

November

Museum Day, Grand Turk. The Turks & Caicos National Museum celebrates the anniversary of its opening with lots of activities, including song and dance performances by local schoolchildren. For more information, go to **www.tcmuseum. org** or call ✆ **649/946-2160.** Saturday closest to November 21 (which is the day the museum opened in 1991).

Turks & Caicos Conch Festival, Providenciales. The conchetition gets fiercer every year as local restaurants vie to win top honors for best conch concoctions, including conch chowder, conch curry, and conch salad, to name just a few of the contested dishes. Just in its third year, the conch festival is a popular celebration, with music, food, conch-blowing, and a great seaside Blue Hills location. For more information, go to **www.conch festival.com**. Last Saturday in November.

December

Christmas Tree-Lighting Ceremony, Providenciales. The Providenciales Kiwanis Club invites the public to the Downtown Ball Park for Christmas festivities, including a choir and a visit from Santa Claus. Mid-December.

Island Thyme Annual Xmas Tree Ornament Competition, Salt Cay. The best handmade ornaments are judged (and prizes awarded to) at this popular and always festive restaurant. For more information, call ℂ **649/946-6977.** Call for exact date.

Old Year's Night, island-wide. Services at churches all over the country ring out the old and ring in the new. December 31.

7 Travel Insurance

Check your existing insurance policies and credit card coverage before you buy travel insurance. You may already be covered for lost luggage, canceled tickets, and/or medical expenses.

The cost of travel insurance varies widely, depending on the cost and length of your trip, your age and health, and the type of trip you're taking, but expect to pay between 5% and 8% of the vacation itself. You can get estimates from various providers through **Insure-MyTrip.com.** Enter your trip cost and dates, your age, and other information for prices from more than a dozen companies.

TRIP-CANCELLATION INSURANCE   Trip-cancellation insurance helps you get your money back if you have to back out of a trip, if you have to go home early, or if your travel supplier goes bankrupt. Permissible reasons for cancellation can range from sickness to natural disasters to the State Department declaring your destination unsafe for travel.

For information, contact one of the following recommended insurers: **Access America** (ℂ 866/807-3982; www.accessamerica. com), **Travel Guard International** (ℂ 800/826-4919; www.travel guard.com), **Travel Insured International** (ℂ 800/243-3174; www. travelinsured.com), or **Travelex Insurance Services** (ℂ 888/457-4602; www.travelex-insurance.com).

MEDICAL INSURANCE   For travel overseas, most health plans (including Medicare and Medicaid) do not provide coverage, and the ones that do often require you to pay for services upfront and reimburse you only after you return home. As a safety net, you may want to buy travel medical insurance, particularly if you're traveling to a remote or high-risk area where emergency evacuation is a possible scenario. If you require additional medical insurance, try **MEDEX Assistance** (© 410/453-6300; www.medexassist.com) or **Travel Assistance International** (© 800/821-2828; www.travel assistance.com; for general information on services, call the company's Worldwide Assistance Services, Inc., at © 800/777-8710).

LOST-LUGGAGE INSURANCE   On flights within the U.S., checked baggage is covered up to $2,500 per ticketed passenger. On international flights (including U.S. portions of international trips), baggage coverage is limited to approximately $9.07 per pound, up to approximately $635 per checked bag. If you plan to check items more valuable than the standard liability, see if your homeowner's policy covers your valuables, get baggage insurance as part of your comprehensive travel-insurance package, or buy Travel Guard's "BagTrak" product.

If your luggage is lost, immediately file a lost-luggage claim at the airport, detailing the luggage contents. Most airlines require that you report delayed, damaged, or lost baggage within 4 hours of arrival. The airlines are required to deliver luggage, once found, directly to your house or destination free of charge.

8 Health & Safety

The Turks & Caicos Islands are great for the soul but may be even better for the body. The TCI has no poisonous snakes or spiders, no malaria or other tropical diseases, is rabies-free, and boasts the Caribbean's lowest crime rate. The wildest animals you'll find here are the islands' "potcake" dogs (see "Take Home a Potcake . . . or Two," below), the homeless canines that roam the islands, and they're generally as gentle as lambs. The waters are protected by a coral reef that rings the islands, so the you won't have to deal with rough surf; in fact, the sea is so gentle and clear (and the sand has so few pebbles and rocks) that this is the perfect spot to teach toddlers and young children how to swim. Still, keep the following suggestions in mind to stay healthy and safe on your trip:

- **Be mindful of the brutal tropical sun.** Wear sunglasses and a hat and use sunscreen liberally. Limit your time on the beach the first day. If you do overexpose yourself, stay out of the sun until you recover. If your exposure is followed by fever or chills, a headache, or a feeling of nausea or dizziness, see a doctor. And keep hydrated: Drink lots of water if you plan to be outside for long periods.

- **Bring insect repellent.** Fortunately, malaria-carrying mosquitoes in the Caribbean are confined largely to Haiti and the Dominican Republic, so you don't have that to worry about. In late afternoon, however, it's a good idea to spray on insect repellent (most restaurants have outdoor seating and often have insect-repellent spray on hand).
- **Be mindful of diving risks.** The Turks & Caicos is a diver's paradise. One of the more serious risks associated with diving is decompression sickness—more commonly known as "the bends." Associated Medical Practices (located in the Medical Building on Leeward Hwy. in Providenciales; © **649/946-4242**) has a dive decompression chamber to treat the bends. *Note:* The treatment is expensive, so be sure to check your dive insurance before you dive.
- **Consider drinking bottled water during your trip.** If you experience diarrhea, moderate your eating habits and drink only bottled water until you recover. If symptoms persist, consult a doctor.
- **Pack prescription medications in your carry-on luggage.** Carry written prescriptions in generic—not brand-name—form, and dispense all prescription medications from their original labeled vials. Many people try to carry drugs such as cocaine via prescription containers; customs officials are well aware of this type of smuggling and often check medication bottles. (**Exception:** Liquid prescriptions *must* be in their original containers, per the latest Transportation Security Administration regulations, and all other liquids, gels, and creams have been banned from carry-on luggage.)
- **Pack an extra pair of contact lenses** (if you wear them), in case you lose one set.

Contact the **International Association for Medical Assistance to Travelers** (**IAMAT;** © **716/754-4883,** or in Canada 416/652-0137; www.iamat.org) for tips on travel and health concerns on the islands you're visiting and lists of local English-speaking doctors. The **United States' Centers for Disease Control and Prevention** (© **800/311-3435;** www.cdc.gov) provides up-to-date information on health hazards by region or country and offers tips on food safety. The website **www.tripprep.com**, sponsored by a consortium of travel-medicine practitioners, may also offer helpful advice.

Take Home a Potcake . . . or Two

The homeless dogs you see roaming the streets of many Caribbean countries generally stay that way: homeless and constantly foraging for food and shelter. The **Turks & Caicos Society for the Prevention of Cruelty to Animals (TCSPCA)** was founded in 2000 to better address the plight of these homeless dogs, here called "potcakes"—the name comes from the food once fed to stray dogs, the caked remains of the bottom of cooking pots. Potcakes may be living in the wild, but they're smart, unflappable, incredibly adaptable, and very loving. Potcakes look like the ultimate mutts, with comically floppy ears and generally tan or black markings, and many a visitor has fallen in love during a stay in the TCI. Along with lobbying the government to adopt animal protection laws and create an animal control unit, the TCSPCA is working to find homes for these dogs—but there are only so many homes on TCI and so many more potcakes. As a result, the TCSPCA is promoting "off-island adoptions," making it easy for visitors to actually carry home a potcake puppy (the TCI has no pet quarantine periods coming in or going out of the country). Every puppy comes with shots and medical certificates and can be carried in the passenger cabins of most airplanes. For more information, contact Susan Blehr, the program director of the TCSPCA, at ⓒ **649/231-3052,** or the island charity set up to improve the lives of TCI potcakes, the **Potcake Foundation** (http://potcakefoundation.com).

WHAT TO DO IF YOU GET SICK AWAY FROM HOME

Finding a good doctor in the Turks & Caicos is not a problem, and most speak English. See the "Fast Facts: The Turks & Caicos Islands" section at the end of this chapter for contact information on **hospitals, emergency numbers,** and **doctors** and **dentists.**

If you suffer from a chronic illness, consult your doctor before your departure. If you worry about getting sick away from home, you might want to consider medical travel insurance (see the section on travel insurance, above).

STAYING SAFE

The TCI is justifiably proud of the fact that it has the lowest crime rate and the highest rate of solved crimes in the Caribbean.

Although crime is minimal in the islands—the locals are deeply offended when someone resorts to robbing people of their possessions—petty theft does take place, so protect your valuables, money, and cameras. Don't flash big wads of money around, especially when you arrive at the airport. Use common sense and be aware of your surroundings at all times.

9 Specialized Travel Resources

TRAVELERS WITH DISABILITIES

Many resorts, condos, and villas in the Turks & Caicos are wheelchair accessible. We've indicated this in the amenities section of the hotel reviews.

Many travel agencies offer customized tours and itineraries for travelers with disabilities. **Flying Wheels Travel** (© 507/451-5005; www.flyingwheelstravel.com) offers escorted tours and cruises that emphasize sports and private tours in minivans with lifts—and has customized itineraries for the Turks & Caicos. **Access-Able Travel Source** (© 303/232-2979; www.access-able.com) offers extensive access information and advice for traveling around the world with disabilities.

Avis Rent a Car has an "Avis Access" program that offers such services as a dedicated 24-hour toll-free number (© 888/879-4273) for customers with special travel needs; special car features such as swivel seats, spinner knobs, and hand controls; and accessible bus service.

Organizations that offer assistance to travelers with disabilities include **MossRehab** (www.mossresourcenet.org), which provides a library of accessible-travel resources online; **SATH** (Society for Accessible Travel & Hospitality; © 212/447-7284; www.sath.org), which offers a wealth of travel resources for all types of disabilities and informed recommendations on destinations, access guides, travel agents, tour operators, vehicle rentals, and companion services; and the **American Foundation for the Blind** (AFB; © 800/232-5463; www.afb.org), a referral resource for the blind or visually impaired that includes information on traveling with Seeing Eye dogs.

The community website **iCan** (www.icanonline.net/channels/travel) has destination guides and several regular columns on accessible travel. Also check out the quarterly magazine *Emerging Horizons* www.emerginghorizons.com); and *Open World* magazine, published by SATH (see above).

GAY & LESBIAN TRAVELERS

The International Gay and Lesbian Travel Association (IGLTA; ☎ **800/448-8550** or 954/776-2626; www.iglta.org) is the trade association for the gay and lesbian travel industry, and offers an online directory of gay- and lesbian-friendly travel businesses; go to its website and click on "Members."

Many agencies offer tours and travel itineraries specifically for gay and lesbian travelers. **Above and Beyond Tours** (☎ **800/397-2681;** www.abovebeyondtours.com) is the exclusive gay and lesbian tour operator for United Airlines. **Now, Voyager** (☎ **800/255-6951;** www.nowvoyager.com) is a well-known San Francisco–based gay-owned and -operated travel service.

Gay.com Travel (☎ **800/929-2268** or 415/644-8044; www.gay.com/travel or www.outandabout.com) is an excellent online successor to the popular *Out & About* print magazine. It provides regularly updated information about gay-owned, gay-oriented, and gay-friendly lodging, dining, sightseeing, nightlife, and shopping establishments in every important destination worldwide.

SENIOR TRAVEL

Members of **AARP** (formerly known as the American Association of Retired Persons), 601 E St. NW, Washington, DC 20049 (☎ **888/687-2277;** www.aarp.org), get discounts on hotels, airfares, and car rentals. AARP offers members a wide range of benefits, including *AARP: The Magazine* and a monthly newsletter. Anyone over 50 can join.

Recommended publications offering travel resources and discounts for seniors include: the quarterly magazine *Travel 50 & Beyond* (www.travel50andbeyond.com); *Travel Unlimited: Uncommon Adventures for the Mature Traveler* (Avalon); *101 Tips for Mature Travelers,* available from Grand Circle Travel (☎ **800/221-2610** or 617/350-7500; www.gct.com); and *Unbelievably Good Deals and Great Adventures That You Absolutely Can't Get Unless You're Over 50* (McGraw-Hill), by Joann Rattner Heilman.

FAMILY TRAVEL

The TCI is a highly recommended family destination. Hotels and resorts by and large welcome families with open arms, and even those with specific adults-only aspects have developed delightful kid-friendly amenities and programs. The gentle, clear, shallow waters and soft-sand beaches of the TCI are particularly attractive for families with toddlers and young children, and older kids will

---

Tips Baby-Equipment Rentals

Most hotels and resorts in Provo are happy to provide cribs, highchairs, and other baby equipment. (Amanyara even provides parents with Diaper Genies and homemade baby food!) If you're renting a villa or condo, however, you may need to rent baby equipment. **Happy Na** (the owner's name is Naomi) has baby-equipment rentals (cribs, car seats, highchairs, and playpens), as well as baby gifts. They're located at Southwinds Plaza on Leeward Highway in Provo (© **649/941-3568** daytime or 649/941-5326 evenings). Cribs rent for $8 to $20 a day. The shop will deliver equipment 7 days a week from 9am to 8pm.

---

have plenty of watersports activities (snorkeling, sailing, parasailing) to keep them happy. One thing you don't find in the TCI, however, is video-game arcades or similar venues where young teens congregate.

10 Planning Your Trip Online

SURFING FOR AIRFARES

The most popular online travel agencies are **Travelocity** (**www. travelocity.com** or www.travelocity.co.uk); **Expedia** (**www.expedia. com**, www.expedia.co.uk, or www.expedia.ca); and **Orbitz** (www. orbitz.com).

In addition, most airlines now offer online-only fares that even their phone agents know nothing about. For the websites of airlines that fly to and from the Turks & Caicos, go to "Getting to Turks & Caicos," later in this chapter.

Other helpful websites for booking airline tickets online include:

- www.biddingfortravel.com
- www.cheapflights.com
- www.hotwire.com
- www.kayak.com
- www.lastminutetravel.com
- www.opodo.co.uk
- www.priceline.com
- www.sidestep.com
- www.site59.com
- www.smartertravel.com

Online Traveler's Toolbox

Veteran travelers usually carry some essential items to make their trips easier. Following is a selection of online tools to bookmark and use.

- **Intellicast** (www.intellicast.com) and **Weather.com** (www. weather.com) give weather forecasts for all 50 states and for cities around the world.
- **MapQuest** (www.mapquest.com), the best of the mapping sites, lets you choose a specific address or destination, and in seconds it will return a map and detailed directions.
- **Travel Warnings** sites (http://travel.state.gov; www.fco. gov.uk/travel; www.voyage.gc.ca; www.dfat.gov.au/consular/advice) report on places where health concerns or unrest might threaten American, British, Canadian, and Australian travelers, respectively. Generally, U.S. warnings are the most paranoid; Australian warnings are the most relaxed.

SURFING FOR HOTELS

In addition to **Travelocity, Expedia, Orbitz, Priceline,** and **Hotwire** (see above), the following websites will help you with booking hotel rooms online:

- www.hotels.com
- www.quickbook.com
- www.travelaxe.com
- www.travelweb.com
- www.tripadvisor.com

It's a good idea to **get a confirmation number** and **make a printout** of any online-booking transaction.

SURFING FOR RENTAL CARS

For booking rental cars online, the best deals are usually found at rental-car company websites, although all the major online travel agencies also offer rental-car reservations services. Priceline and Hotwire work well for rental cars, too; the only "mystery" is which major rental company you get, and for most travelers the difference between Hertz, Avis, and Budget is negligible.

11 Getting to Turks & Caicos

The main point of entry for international flights into the Turks & Caicos is **Providenciales International Airport** (www.provoairport. com); Grand Turk and South Caicos also have international airports. **American Airlines** (✆ 800/433-7300; www.aa.com) is a major carrier throughout the region and flies nonstop flights from New York, Boston, and Miami. Other airlines serving the islands include **Air Canada** (✆ 888/247-2262 in the U.S. and Canada; www.aircanada.ca), which flies nonstop from Toronto; **Air Jamaica** (✆ 800/523-5585; www.airjamaica.com); **Bahamas Air** (✆ 800/ 222-4262; www.bahamasair.com); **British Airways** (✆ 800/AIR-WAYS in the U.S., 0870/850-9850 in the U.K.; www.british airways.com), which flies nonstop from London; **Continental** (✆ 800/231-0856; www.continental.com); **Delta** (✆ 800/221-1212; www.delta.com), which flies nonstop from Atlanta; **Spirit Airlines** (✆ 800/772-7117; www.spiritair.com/welcome.aspx); and **US Airways** (✆ 800/428-4322; www.usairways.com), which flies nonstop from Charlotte.

The Provo airport is small, with limited tourist services. A restaurant, **Gilley's Cafe** (✆ 649/946-4472; open 7 days a week for breakfast and lunch), is near the domestic arrivals and departures area. The international departure lounge has a few duty-free shops—including **Royal Jewels** (✆ 649/946-4699), a small branch of **Maison Creole** (✆ 649/946-4748), and **Turquoise Duty-Free** (✆ 649/946-4536), which sells liquor and Cuban and Dominican cigars—but the only food source is a snack bar with little more substantial than microwave pizza, chips, gum, and drinks. If you have a long wait ahead of you—and hungry kids in tow—consider getting a bite at Gilley's before your flight, or bring food with you.

FLYING FOR LESS: TIPS FOR GETTING THE BEST AIRFARE

Before you do anything else, read the section "Packages for the Independent Traveler," below. But if a package isn't for you and you need to book your airfare on your own, keep in mind these money-saving tips:

- *When* **you fly makes all the difference.** If you fly in late spring, summer, and early fall, you're guaranteed substantial reductions on airfares to the Turks & Caicos. Passengers who can book their tickets long in advance, who can stay over Saturday night, or who fly midweek or at less-trafficked hours

> **Tips** **Don't Fly on a Sunday (or a Saturday)**
>
> If you can possibly swing it, avoid flying in or out of Provo on Saturday or Sunday during peak season. These are the days when the weekly villa or condo rentals turn over, and the modest-size airport is overrun with travelers arriving and departing—the result being that the Customs process at arrivals can be agonizingly slow and the departure lines long and full of (understandably) cranky kids.

may pay a fraction of the full fare. If your schedule is flexible, say so, and ask if you can secure a cheaper fare by changing your flight plans.

- **Search the Internet for cheap fares** (see "Planning Your Trip Online," earlier in this chapter).
- **Keep an eye out for sales.** Check newspapers for advertised discounts or call the airlines directly and ask if any promotional rates or special fares are available. You'll almost never see a sale during the peak winter vacation months of February and March, or during the Thanksgiving or Christmas seasons; but in periods of low-volume travel, you should find a discounted fare. If you already hold a ticket when a sale breaks, it may even pay to exchange your ticket, which usually incurs a $50 to $75 charge. *Note:* The lowest-priced fares are often nonrefundable, require advance purchase of 1 to 3 weeks and a certain length of stay, and carry penalties for changing dates of travel.
- **Consolidators,** also known as bucket shops, are great sources for international tickets. Start by looking in Sunday newspaper travel sections; U.S. travelers should focus on the *New York Times, Los Angeles Times,* and *Miami Herald.* U.K. travelers should search in the *Independent,* the *Guardian,* or the *Observer.* For less-developed destinations, small travel agencies that cater to immigrant communities in large cities often have the best deals. *Beware:* Bucket-shop tickets are usually nonrefundable or rigged with stiff cancellation penalties, often as high as 50% to 75% of the ticket price, and some put you on charter airlines, which may leave at inconvenient times and experience delays. Several reliable consolidators are worldwide and available online. **STA Travel** has been the world's lead consolidator for students since purchasing Council Travel, but their fares are competitive for travelers of all ages. **ELTExpress (Flights.com)**

Tips   Getting Through the Airport

- Arrive at the airport 1 hour before a domestic flight and 2 hours before an international flight; if you show up late, tell an airline employee and he or she will probably whisk you to the front of the line.
- Beat the ticket-counter lines by using airport electronic kiosks or even online check-in from your home computers, from where you can print out boarding passes in advance. Curbside check-in is also a good way to avoid lines.
- Bring a current, government-issued photo ID such as a driver's license or passport. Children under 18 do not need government-issued photo IDs for flights within the U.S., but they do for international flights to most countries.
- Speed up security by removing your jacket and shoes before you're screened. In addition, remove metal objects such as big belt buckles. If you've got metallic body parts, a note from your doctor can prevent a long chat with the security screeners.
- Use a TSA-approved lock for your checked luggage. Look for Travel Sentry certified locks at luggage or travel shops and Brookstone stores (or online at www. brookstone.com).
- Follow new Transportation Security Administration (TSA) regulations when packing your carry-on luggage. Because of a terrorist plot thwarted in August 2006, all beverages, oils, gels, creams, and aerosol cans have been banned, with just a few exceptions for liquid prescriptions and baby formulas. Log onto www.tsa.gov/travelers/index.shtm for details.

(© **800/TRAV-800**; www.eltexpress.com) has excellent fares worldwide, particularly to Europe. They also have "local" websites in 12 countries. **FlyCheap** (© **800/FLYCHEAP**; www.1800flycheap.com), owned by package-holiday megalith MyTravel, has especially good fares to sunny destinations. **Air Tickets Direct** (© **800/778-3447**; www.airticketsdirect.com) is based in Montreal and leverages the currently weak Canadian dollar for low fares.

- **Join frequent-flier clubs.** Frequent-flier membership doesn't cost a cent, but it does entitle you to better seats, faster response to phone inquiries, and prompter service if your luggage is stolen or your flight is canceled or delayed, or if you want to change your seat. And you don't have to fly to earn points; **frequent-flier credit cards** can earn you thousands of miles for doing your everyday shopping. With more than 70 mileage awards programs on the market, consumers have never had more options. Investigate the program details of your favorite airlines before you sink points into any one. Consider which airlines have hubs in the airport nearest you, and, of those carriers, which have the most advantageous alliances, given your most common routes. To play the frequent-flier game to your best advantage, consult Randy Petersen's **Inside Flyer** (www.insideflyer.com). Petersen and friends review all the programs in detail and post regular updates on changes in policies and trends.

12 Packages for the Independent Traveler

For value-conscious travelers, packages are often the smart way to go because they can save you a ton of money. Especially in the Caribbean, package tours are *not* the same thing as escorted tours. You'll be on your own, but in most cases, a package to the Turks & Caicos will include airfare, hotel, and transportation to and from the airport—and it'll cost you less than just the hotel alone if you booked it yourself.

You'll find an amazing array of packages to the Turks & Caicos, largely involving stays in Provo. Several big **online travel agencies**—Expedia, Travelocity, Orbitz, Site59, and Lastminute.com—do a brisk business in packages. Remember to comparison shop among at least three different operators, and always compare apples to apples.

One good source of package deals is the airlines themselves. Most major airlines offer air/land packages, including **American Airlines Vacations** (✆ 800/321-2121; www.aavacations.com), **Delta Vacations** (✆ 800/221-6666; www.deltavacations.com), **Continental Airlines Vacations** (✆ 800/301-3800; www.covacations.com), and **United Vacations** (✆ 888/854-3899; www.unitedvacations.com).

Of course, don't forget to check the **hotel or resort websites** for very desirable package deals, especially in the off season. No, these packages rarely include airfares, but they're packed with extra amenities (or a night free) if you book a block of vacation time, say, 5 or 7 days. These packages are often built around themes, such as Romance Week, Spa Escape, or Island Getaway, and often include meals, spa treatments, or watersports excursions along with the lodging. Similarly, in Grand Turk, where the scuba diving is world-class, most hotels offer dive packages—competitively priced hotel/dive vacations.

13 Getting Around the Turks & Caicos Islands

Your most likely point of entry into the Turks & Caicos Islands will be the Providenciales International Airport. Depending on your final destination, from there you will take a taxi or rental car or hop on another flight.

Note: In general, addresses have no street numbers, more typically just designations like "Leeward Highway," "Lower Bight Road," or simply "Providenciales."

For more information on getting around in Grand Turk and Salt Cay, go to chapter 6.

GETTING AROUND PROVIDENCIALES
FROM THE AIRPORT

Most hotels arrange **transfers** to and from the airport; otherwise, **taxis** are on hand to meet arriving flights. If for some reason none are around, call the **Provo Taxi Association** (© 649/946-5481). Cabs are metered and rates set by the government—but not all taxi drivers turn on their meters, so it's a good idea to negotiate the fare before you leave the airport—or anytime, for that matter. Expect to pay around $22 to $25 (plus tip) per couple (additional person $7.50) for a taxi ride from the airport to the Grace Bay area. Most taxis are vans equipped to carry more than one group of passengers, so it stands to reason that the more people onboard, the lower the rate per couple.

Because the island is so large and its hotels and restaurants are so far-flung, you might find a **rental car** useful on Providenciales, but be warned: Renting a car on the TCI is not cheap. The airport has several rental-car agencies at the airport (see "Rental Cars," below).

TAXIS

If you decide to forgo a rental car, you may find yourself needing a taxi every now and then, whether to get back to your hotel after dinner out, for example, or if you simply don't feel like waiting for the Gecko Shuttle to show up, particularly at night, when the shuttle is on an abbreviated schedule. Taxis are plentiful on Provo, but there are no designated taxi stands. If you need a taxi, you'll have to call one; try the **Provo Taxi Association** (see above). We also highly recommend Mackey Missick of **C&M Taxi Service** (© **649/242-2704** or 649/243-6978) and Wayne Outten of **Outten's Taxi & Tour Service** (© **649/241-4098**). If you find another taxi driver you like, ask for his or her card or jot down the number on the side of the van, and avail yourself of his or her services throughout your trip (taxi drivers are also happy to show you around the island—for a fee negotiated upfront, of course). Some Provo hotels even include complimentary transportation around the Grace Bay area in their rates. Otherwise, most places are happy to call a taxi for you.

RENTAL CARS

Three major U.S.-based car-rental agencies with a franchise in the Turks & Caicos Islands are **Budget,** with two Provo locations: the airport and Downtown Provo, in the Town Centre Mall (© **800/ 472-3325** in the U.S., or 649/946-4079, -5400; www.budget rentacar.com); **Avis,** with a branch at the airport (© **800/331-1212** in the U.S. and Canada, or 649/946-4705; www.avis.com); and **Hertz** affiliate **Mystique Car Rental,** on Old Airport Road, 2 minutes from the airport (© **649/941-3910;** www.hertztci.com). Cars rent for $54 to $225 a day (depending on the vehicle); collision-damage insurance costs $10 to $12 a day. The local government will collect a $16 tax for each rental contract, regardless of the number of days you keep the car.

If you'd like to try your luck with a local agency, call one of the following: **Turks & Caicos National Car Rental** (© **649/946-4701**), which has a branch at the Airport Plaza on Airport Road (2 min. from the airport); **Rent a Buggy** (© **649/946-4158**) on Leeward Highway, near Central Square; **Provo Rent A Car** (© **649/ 946-4404**), in Grace Bay Plaza; or **Scooter Bob's,** Turtle Cove Marina; (© **649/946-4684;** www.provo.net/scooter/), which rents jeeps, vans, and SUVs. Most of these agencies offer free pickup and drop-off. Rates average from $40 to $90 per day, plus a $15 government tax.

In the British tradition, **cars on all the islands drive on the left.** You only need a valid driver's license from your home country to rent a vehicle.

GECKO SHUTTLE

These red air-conditioned vans have been a colorful and smart addition to the transportation options along Provo's Grace Bay. The

Renting a Car in Provo: Pros & Cons

Many visitors wonder whether renting a car is the thing to do when in Provo. Some things to consider:

Pros:

- You can easily tour the island, go to shops, and eat out and not have to walk long distances to get places, worry about relying on taxis, or wait for the Gecko Shuttle coming and going (especially in the evenings).
- You can pick up supplies and food (especially if you have self-catering capabilities) from the Graceway IGA and other food suppliers with ease.
- Taxis can be pricey!

Cons:

- If you're North American, you have to quickly master the nuances of left-side driving and navigating roundabouts.
- Parking is limited at many resorts. Some, like the Grace Bay Club, offset this issue by providing complimentary transportation anywhere around the Grace Bay area for guests without cars.
- Most, if not all, tour operators include hotel pickup as part of their excursion packages.
- Bike riding is an ideal way to get around and perfectly meshes with the eco-friendly island vibe. But if your hotel or resort doesn't offer complimentary bikes (or has limited supplies), you're out of luck in the Grace Bay area—currently no one rents bikes (although scooters are rentable; see below).
- The Gecko Shuttle stops almost everywhere you need to go on the island—and taxis are plentiful. Plus, more cars mean more congestion.
- Rental cars can be pricey!

handsome little Gecko (www.thegecko.tc) makes regular stops at just about every resort, shopping plaza, and restaurant from Ocean Club East to the Turtle Cove area (with additional stops at Central Sq. and the Graceway IGA grocery store), and with a daily or weekly pass, you can hop on or hop off at your leisure. The Gecko is a great option for people with self-catering capabilities and no car—they can use the shuttle to shop for groceries at the IGA. On the negative side, if you miss a shuttle stop, you'll have to wait 30 minutes for the next Gecko to show up. In addition, the Gecko can be slow going, stopping everywhere along the way (but hey, you're on island time and sightseeing to boot!), and it's a little pricey (daily passes $11 adults and children 5 and over, $5.50 children under 5; weekly passes $55 adults and children 5 and over, $33 children under 5). You can also buy single tokens (for one ride) for $4. In high season the Gecko runs from 10am to 11pm Sunday through Wednesday, and 10am to 2am Thursday through Saturday; shuttle runs end earlier in the evenings in low season. No cash is taken on the shuttle— you must have a pass or token to ride. Passes and tokens are sold at most hotel desks and selected shops.

BICYCLES & SCOOTERS
Bicycling is an ideal way to get around the flat Grace Bay area, especially now that the roads have been beautifully paved with sidewalks running on both sides. Many resorts, including Royal West Indies and the Sands at Grace Bay, offer complimentary bikes for their guests. Unfortunately, at this time there is no place to rent bikes in the area.

In addition to cars, jeeps, and SUVs, **Scooter Bob's** (Turtle Cove Marina; ✆ **649/946-4684;** www.provo.net/scooter/) rents two-passenger Yamaha scooters for $49 a day ($45 a day for 5 days or more). Advance reservations are required.

You can also rent scooters and bikes at www.tonyscarrental.com.

ON FOOT
The 19km (12 miles) of Grace Bay Beach make for lovely strolls, and the newly paved roads along Grace Bay have sidewalks, so getting around on foot is much easier than before. But once you get started, particularly with the tropical sun beating down, keep in mind that the distances are longer than they appear on a map.

GETTING TO THE OTHER ISLANDS & GETTING AROUND
If your final destination is any of the other TCI islands, you will be taking either a **domestic flight** on a small plane from the Provo airport or traveling **by boat** (generally from Leeward Marina, on Provo's northeast coast, about 20 min. from the airport; to get there you'll need to take a taxi from the airport if your hotel doesn't offer airport transfers).

CAICOS CAYS

The Caicos Cays are reachable by **boat** or **private plane** or **air taxi;**
Pine Cay has a tiny airstrip that's used by island homeowners and
Meridian Club guests. Guests staying 7 nights or more at Pine Cay's
Meridian Club enjoy complimentary air-taxi transfers from the
Provo airport or van transfers and boat transfers to Leeward Marina.
Guests staying on Parrot Cay enjoy complimentary transfers from
the Provo airport and boat transfers from Leeward Marina. A num-
ber of the uninhabited cays, such as Fort George Cay and Little
Water Cay, are destinations on many local tour-boat operators' half-
day and full-day beach excursions.

NORTH CAICOS

You can fly to the North Caicos airstrip on **Air Turks & Caicos**
(formerly Interisland Airways) (© **649/941-5481;** www.airturks
andcaicos.com) or the charter company **Global Airways** (© **649/
941-3222;** www.globalairways.tc); daily flights costs $65 round-trip
and take approximately 10 minutes. Otherwise, you can get here by
chartering a water-taxi from one of the many tour-boat operators in
the area; try **J&B Tours** (© **649/946-5047;** www.jbtours.com;
$200 one-way; up to 6–8 people) or **Big Blue Unlimited** (© **649/
946-5034;** http://bigblue.tc; $100 per person; three-person mini-
mum); the trip takes around 35 minutes. For ground transportation, call **Charlie's Taxi** (© **649/946-7167**).

MIDDLE CAICOS

You can fly to the minuscule Middle Caicos airstrip on **Air Turks &
Caicos** (www.airturksandcaicos.com) or the charter company **Global
Airways** (© **649/941-3222;** www.globalairways.tc); daily flights cost
$85 round-trip and take approximately 15 minutes. You can take
the ferry from North Caicos (see above). For ground transportation,
island and cave tours, boat excursions, and fishing expeditions, call

---

Tips **Ferry Between North & Middle Caicos**

Weekend ferry service between Bottle Creek on North Caicos
and Middle Caicos runs Saturday beginning at 8am through
early afternoon. The ride is 30 minutes each way, and the
ferry holds two vehicles ($20 round-trip).

Middle Caicos native and guide extraordinaire **Cardinal Arthur** (© **649/946-6107;** cellphone 649/241-0730).

SOUTH CAICOS

SkyKing (© **649/941-3136;** www.skyking.tc) flies daily to South Caicos from Provo; flights cost $126 (3-day advance purchase; otherwise, $146) and take approximately 20 minutes. Taxis are available at the airport.

GRAND TURK

Most people fly into Providenciales and then take a short flight on a domestic airline into Grand Turk International Airport (also known as J.A.G.S. McCartney International Airport). Several daily flights between Provo and Grand Turk are offered by **SkyKing** (© **649/941-3136;** www.skyking.tc) and **Air Turks & Caicos** (© **649/941-5481** or 649/946-1667 on Grand Turk; www.airturks andcaicos.com). The flight from Provo to Grand Turk takes 20 minutes and costs approximately $135 round-trip.

As of 2006, **Spirit Airlines** was offering direct flights (Sun only) from Fort Lauderdale, Florida, to Grand Turk (© **800/772-7117;** www.spiritair.com/welcome.aspx).

On Grand Turk you can rent cars (as well as scooters, bicycles, and snorkeling gear) at **Tony's Car Rental** (Grand Turk International Airport; © **649/964-1979;** www.tonyscarrental.com). Cars and jeeps rent for from $70 to $95 a day, scooter rentals cost $40 a day, and bike rentals are $20 a day. Tony's also offers scooter tours of the island.

Taxis are always available at the Grand Turk airport, and drivers are more than happy to give visitors a tour of the island; expect to pay around $50 for a 45-minute island tour.

For more information on getting to and getting around Grand Turk, see chapter 6.

SALT CAY

Only two airlines have planes small enough to land and take off from the tiny runway at the Salt Cay airport, but at press time the government had earmarked considerable funds to lengthen and resurface the airstrip and upgrade South Dock; work was to begin immediately and may be completed by the time this guide is in the stores—once finished, airlines like SkyKing (see contact information above) can deliver visitors to this delightful island. Currently, however, only **Air Turks & Caicos** (℗ **649/941-5481** or 649/946-6940 or -6906 on Salt Cay; www.airturksandcaicos.com) and **Global Airways** charters (℗ **649/941-3222;** www.globalairways.tc) fly to Salt Cay.

Air Turks & Caicos offers regularly scheduled flights daily between Provo and Grand Turk (see above), and then three flights a day from Grand Turk to Salt Cay; the Grand Turk–Salt Cay leg takes under 10 minutes and costs $50 round-trip. The one daily flight from Provo to Salt Cay takes 30 minutes and costs $165.

Contact Global for schedules, which can change daily.

A government-subsidized **ferry** runs between Grand Turk and Salt Cay, weather permitting, every Wednesday and Friday (leaving from South Dock—the island's *only* dock, by the way—at Salt Cay at 7:30am and returning at 2:30pm). The trip takes an hour and costs $12. You can also hire a **private boat operator** to take you between Salt Cay and Grand Turk (as long as the seas aren't too rough). Contact Nathan Smith (see below) or hire a boat charter with **Salt Cay Adventure Tours** (℗ **649/946-6909;** www.saltcay tours.com). **Cruise-ship passengers** who arrive in Grand Turk can also contact Salt Cay Adventures to arrange day trips to Salt Cay.

No one needs a car to get around Salt Cay, which has more donkeys than cars to begin with; it's the perfect place for getting around on foot, by bike, or by golf cart. **Nathan Smith,** the "unofficial mayor of Salt Cay," not only offers taxi service from the airport but rents golf carts and bikes (and offers tours of all kinds, including snorkeling and troll fishing for tuna). Contact Smith's Golf-Cart & Bike Rental, located next to the Salt Cay Divers dive shop (℗ **649/946-6928** or cellphone 649/231-4856; two-seater golf-carts $50/day, $280/week; four-seaters $60/day, $350/week; bikes $10/day; credit cards accepted).

For more information on getting to and getting around Salt Cay, see chapter 6.

14 Internet Access Away from Home
WITHOUT YOUR OWN COMPUTER

Many **hotels** and **resorts** in the TCI feature "libraries" or small business centers where guests have complimentary use of computers with high-speed Internet access. The number of computers available is often limited, however, and you may have to wait your turn to use one.

WITH YOUR OWN COMPUTER

The wireless world (Wi-Fi) is coming to the Turks & Caicos Islands; hotels like Amanyara already have resort-wide wireless Internet access. For dial-up access, most business-class hotels offer dataports for laptop modems. In addition, major Internet service providers (ISPs) have **local access numbers** around the world, allowing you to go online by placing a local call. The **iPass** network also has dial-up numbers around the world. You'll have to sign up with an iPass provider, who will then tell you how to set up your computer for your destination(s). For a list of iPass providers, go to www.ipass. com and click on "Individuals Buy Now." One solid provider is **i2roam** (www.i2roam.com; ℭ **866/811-6209** or 920/235-0475).

Wherever you go, bring a **connection kit** of the right power and phone adapters, a spare phone cord, and a spare Ethernet network cable—or find out whether your hotel supplies them to guests.

15 Getting Married in Turks & Caicos

As TCI Chief Minister Michael Misick proved when he married Hollywood starlet LisaRaye McCoy (star of the UPN comedy *All of Us*) in 2006 in a celebrity-studded wedding at Amanyara, the Turks & Caicos Islands are a hot destination-wedding spot. You can get married barefoot on the beach, in a ballroom at a luxury resort, on a sailboat, or in one of the island's colorful churches, to name a few choice scenarios. An increasing number of resorts and tour operators are equipped to handle weddings soup-to-nuts. Here is a sampling of options:

- **Sail Provo** (www.sailprovo.com) can organize a wedding on one of its large catamarans or on a secluded beach, with all the trimmings, for up to 100 people.
- **The Palms** resort offers customized wedding services and your choice of ceremony locations (on the beach, in the Palms Courtyard—which was featured in the Aug 2005 issue of *Modern Bride*—or in the Messel Ballroom) and reception locations (the Messel Ballroom, on the beachside wooden deck, or in the courtyard).
- **Beaches Turks & Caicos** (ℭ **800/SANDALS**) marries couples on a regular basis—in high season as many as *80 couples a month*. It's big business for Beaches, and they take it very seriously, with an on-site wedding coordinator and complete wedding packages to choose from.

You need to meet the following legal requirements to marry in the TCI: You will need to bring a passport, a copy of your birth certificate, proof of status from your place of residence (if single, a sworn affidavit), and a divorce decree if you're divorced. You will need to pay a $100 license fee and $20 for a copy of the marriage certificate. You must be on island for 48 hours to establish residency, and the marriage license takes 48 hours to process. *Note:* If you plan to marry in the one of the island churches, you may need proof of membership.

The Turks & Caicos Islands marriage certificate is legally recognized in the U.S., Canada, and the U.K. For more details, contact **The Registry of Births, Deaths and Marriages** on Front Street at ℭ **649/946-2800** in Grand Turk (the Registry also has an office in Provo at ℭ **649/946-5350**).

16 Tips on Accommodations

SAVING ON YOUR HOTEL ROOM

The rates given in this book are only "rack rates"—that is, the officially posted rate that you'd be given if you just walked in off the street. Almost no one actually pays them. Always ask about packages and discounts. Think of the rates in this book as guidelines to help you comparison shop.

The high season in the Turks & Caicos is the winter season, roughly from the middle of December through the middle of April. Hotels charge their highest rates during the winter season, and you'll need to make reservations months in advance to snag a room at your favorite hotel or resort during this peak period. The Christmas holidays have become big business for TCI lodgings, and you may need to reserve a year in advance for a room during this time.

The off season in the TCI is the rest of the year—although the so-called "shoulder seasons," roughly late spring and late fall (after hurricane season is over)—are increasingly popular. Still, outside the traditional high season, expect rates to fall, sometimes dramatically in the summer.

WATCH OUT FOR THOSE EXTRAS! The government imposes a flat 10% occupancy tax, applicable to all hotels, guesthouses, and restaurants in the 40-island chain. When booking a room, ask whether the price you've been quoted includes the tax. That will avoid an unpleasant surprise when it comes time to pay the bill.

Furthermore, many hotels routinely add 10% to 12% for "service," even if you didn't see much evidence of it. That means that with tax and service, some bills are 17% or even 25% higher than the price that was originally quoted to you! Naturally, you need to determine just how much the hotel, guesthouse, or inn plans to add to your bill at the end of your stay, and whether it's included in the initial price.

That's not all. Some hotels slip in little hidden extras that mount quickly. For example, it's common for many places to quote rates that include a continental breakfast. Should you prefer ham and eggs, you will pay extra charges. If you request special privileges, like extra towels for the beach or laundry done in a hurry, surcharges may mount. It pays to watch those extras and to ask questions before you commit.

One of the biggest extras is phone charges. Try to avoid making international calls from your hotel phone—you'll be charged around $2.10 a minute, depending on the time of day, which can add up quickly. Many hotels also have fees for local calls, sometimes $1 and up. If you have a GSM cellphone with international roaming capabilities, you're in business; otherwise, you may want to consider renting a cellphone or buying a prepaid cellphone when you're on island. See "Calling Home," earlier in this chapter.

WHAT THE ABBREVIATIONS MEAN   Rate sheets often have these classifications:

- **MAP (Modified American Plan)** usually means room, breakfast, and dinner, unless the room rate has been quoted separately, in which case it means only breakfast and dinner.
- **CP (Continental Plan)** includes room and a light breakfast.
- **EP (European Plan)** means room only.
- **AP (American Plan)** includes your room plus three meals a day.

HOTELS & RESORTS   Many budget travelers assume they can't afford the big hotels and resorts. But there are so many packages out there (see the section "Packages for the Independent Traveler," earlier in this chapter) and so many advertised sales during the low season that you might be pleasantly surprised at what you can get. And many hotels offer upgrades whenever they have a big block of rooms to fill and few reservations.

ALL-INCLUSIVE RESORTS   The ideal all-inclusive is just that— a place where *everything*—meals, drinks, and most watersports—is

All the Rage: Condo Hotels

In the Turks & Caicos, the buzzword in resort development is **condo hotels.** Many, if not most, of the resorts on Grace Bay are fully or partially condo hotels. Condo hotels are nothing but hotels whose units are sold to individual owners, usually even before the hotel is built. When the owner is not using the unit, he or she shares in the income when the hotel management rents it out to guests. This is a popular concept in the TCI for a number of reasons, one of which is the favorable financial conditions here for international investors, large and small, including no property taxes, capital gains taxes, or sales taxes.

included. In the Turks & Caicos, only two resorts bill themselves as all-inclusive: **Beaches** and **Club Med Turkoise.** The all-inclusive market is geared to the active traveler who likes organized entertainment, lots of sports and workouts at fitness centers, and lots of food and drink—and neither Beaches nor Club Med fails to come through in these categories.

In the 1990s, so many competitors entered the all-inclusive market that the term means different things to the different resorts that embrace this marketing strategy. At Beaches and Club Med, all meals, drinks, and gratuities are included, for example, but you'll have to pay for extras such as certain spa treatments and optional scuba-diving services. It's a good idea to find out before you book just what is included and what is not.

The all-inclusives have a reputation for being expensive, but to many people not having to "pay as you go" or deal with gratuities—not to mention knowing exactly what you're paying for—is liberating and worth the money. If you're looking for ways to cut costs with an all-inclusive, the trick is to travel in off-peak periods, which doesn't always mean just from mid-April to mid-December. If you want a winter vacation at an all-inclusive, choose the month of January—not February or the Christmas holidays, when prices are at their all-year high. The resorts also regularly offer special packages for weeklong stays; check the websites for the latest offerings.

GUESTHOUSES/INNS   An entirely different type of accommodations is the guesthouse. In the Caribbean the term "guesthouse" can mean anything. Sometimes so-called guesthouses are really like simple motels built around swimming pools. Others are small individual cottages, with their own kitchenettes, constructed around a main building in which you'll often find a bar and a restaurant that serves local food. Still others are more like small inns, often with private bathrooms, luxury linens, and boutique amenities. The guesthouse or inn usually represents good value, simply because it does not have the full-service amenities of a resort or hotel.

Unfortunately, Provo has few if any guesthouses and small inns, but you can find them on the other islands, particularly Grand Turk.

RENTING A CONDO, VILLA, OR HOUSE   Particularly if you're a family or a group of friends, a "housekeeping holiday" can be one of the least expensive ways to vacation in the Turks & Caicos, and if you like privacy and independence, it's a good way to go. Accommodations with kitchens are now available on nearly all the islands. Some are individual cottages, others are condo complexes with swimming pools, and many others are private homes that owners rent out. Many (though not all) places include maid service, and you're given fresh linens as well.

In the simpler rentals, doing your own cooking and laundry or even your own maid service may not be your idea of a good time in the sun, but it saves money—a lot of money. The savings, especially for a family of three to six people, or two or three couples, can range from 50% to 60% of what a hotel would cost. Groceries are sometimes priced 35% to 60% higher than on the U.S. mainland, as nearly all foodstuffs have to be imported, but even so, preparing your own food will be a lot cheaper than dining at restaurants.

There are also a number of quite lavish homes for rent for which you can spend a lot and stay in the lap of luxury in a prime beachfront setting. Many villas have a staff, or at least a maid who comes in a few days a week, and they also provide the essentials for home life, including linens and housewares. Condos usually come with a reception desk and are often comparable to a suite in a big resort hotel. Nearly all condo complexes have pools (some more than one). Like condos, villas range widely in price.

You'll have to approach these rental properties with a certain sense of independence. There may or may not be a front desk to answer your questions, and you'll have to plan your own watersports.

For a list of agencies that arrange rentals in Providenciales, see a few recommended options below. If you're looking for rentals in North or Middle Caicos, you can ask the Turks & Caicos Tourist

Board for good suggestions. For villa rentals in Grand Turk and Salt Cay, see chapter 6.

Make your reservations well in advance. Here are a few agencies that rent in Provo:

- **Prestigious Properties** (© **649/946-4379;** www.prestigious properties.com) offers a variety of villas, condos, and single-family residences.
- **Seafeathers Villas** (© **649/941-5703;** www.seafeathers.com) has a variety of beachfront villas, cottages, and condos, many with private pools and beach or oceanfront. Chefs, maids, and babysitters are also available on request.
- **Ocean Point & North Shore Villas** (© **649/941-5703;** www. oceanpointvillas.com) has lovely deluxe villas ranging in size from two to seven bedrooms in the strictly residential neighborhood of Ocean Point and on the North Shore near Turtle Cove.

LANDING THE BEST ROOM

Somebody has to get the best room in the house—it might as well be you. You can start by joining hotels' frequent-guest programs, which may make you eligible for upgrades. A hotel-branded credit card usually gives its owner "silver" or "gold" status in frequent-guest programs for free.

Always ask about a corner room. They're often larger and quieter, with more windows and light, and they often cost the same as standard rooms. When you make your reservation, ask if the hotel is renovating; if it is, request a room away from the construction. Ask about nonsmoking rooms, rooms with views, and rooms with twin or queen- or king-size beds. If you're a light sleeper, request a quiet room away from vending machines, elevators, restaurants, bars, and discos. Ask for one of the rooms that have been most recently renovated or redecorated.

If you aren't happy with your room when you arrive, say so. If another room is available, most lodgings will be willing to accommodate you. Ask the following questions before you book a room:

- What's the view like? Cost-conscious travelers may be willing to pay less for a back room facing the parking lot, especially if they don't plan to spend much time in their room.
- Does the room have air-conditioning or ceiling fans? Do the windows open? If they do, and the nighttime entertainment takes place alfresco, you may want to find out when showtime is over.

- What's included in the price? Your room may be moderately priced, but if you're charged for beach chairs, towels, sports equipment, and other amenities, you could end up spending more than you bargained for.
- How far is the room from the beach and other amenities? If it's far, is there transportation to and from the beach?

FAST FACTS: The Turks & Caicos Islands

Area Code The area/country code for the TCI is **649**.

ATMs/ABMs First Caribbean (connected to the PLUS ABM network) has 24-hour ABM service at the main branches of its bank in Provo and Grand Turk (see "Banks," below). Scotiabank (connected to Cirrus) has ATMs at its main locations on Provo and Grand Turk and two additional ATMs in Provo, one in the Ports of Call shopping center on Grace Bay Road and the other next to the Graceway IGA on Leeward Highway (all open 24 hr. a day).

Banks Branches of the **First Caribbean International Bank** (✆ **649/946-2831**) and **Scotiabank** (✆ **649/946-4750**) are at convenient and central locations on Provo (Leeward Hwy.) and Grand Turk (Front St.).

Business Hours Most shops are open Monday to Saturday from 10am to 6pm, but hours vary. Banks are generally open Monday to Thursday from 8am to 2:30pm and Friday from 8:30am to 4:30pm. Most grocery stores are open 7 days a week but do not sell liquor, beer, or wine on Sunday.

Currency The **U.S. dollar** is the official currency.

Dentists **Dental Services Limited** is located in the Medical Building on Leeward Highway in Providenciales (✆ **649/946-4321**; www.dentist.tc).

Doctors **Dr. Sam Slattery** sees patients at the **Grace Bay Medical Center** (Neptune Plaza, Allegro Rd., Providenciales; ✆ **649/941-5252**). **Associated Medical Practices** is located in the Medical Building on Leeward Highway in Providenciales (✆ **649/946-4242**). Associated also has a dive decompression chamber.

Drugstores There are two full-service pharmacies: **Grace Bay Pharmacy,** located on Dolphin Drive between Grace Bay Road and the Leeward Highway (✆ **649/946-8242**), and **Island**

Pharmacy, in the Medical Building on Leeward Highway in Providenciales (✆ **649/946-4150**).

Electricity The electric current on the islands is 120 volts, 60 cycles, AC. European appliances will need adapters.

Emergencies Call ✆ **911** or **999** for an **ambulance,** to report a **fire,** or to contact the **police.**

Hospitals/Medical Facilities **Grace Bay Medical Center** is an urgent-care medical facility in Providenciales (Neptune Plaza, Allegro Rd., Providenciales; ✆ **649/941-5252;** for emergencies call ✆ **649/231-0525**). **Grand Turk Hospital** is on Hospital Road in Grand Turk (✆ **649/946-2040**). The other islands have community clinics.

Internet Access Most resorts and hotels have some sort of Internet access. You can also access the Internet at **TCIonline Internet Café** (Ports of Call shopping center, Provo; ✆ **649/941-4711**) or **CompTCI** (Suzy Turn Plaza, Provo; ✆ **649/941-4266;** www.comptci.com). Prices are around $10 an hour.

Language The official language is English.

Pets All you need to bring a pet onto the islands is a signed veterinary certificate (dated within 1 month of travel) stating that the animal is free of contagious or infectious disease and up-to-date on his or her rabies and distemper vaccinations. There is no quarantine period for incoming pets.

Post Office The Provo Post Office and Philatelic Bureau is located downtown at the corner of Airport Road. It's open Monday to Thursday from 8am to 4pm and Friday from 8am to 3:30pm. The Grand Turk Post Office is located on Front Street in Cockburn Town. It's open Monday to Friday from 8am to 4pm.

Taxes There is a departure tax of $35, payable when you leave the islands (it's often included in the cost of your airfare). The government collects a 10% occupancy tax, applicable to all hotels, guesthouses, and restaurants in the 40-island chain. Hotels often add a 10% to 15% service charge on top of the government tax.

Telephone To call Turks and Caicos, dial **1** and then the number. The country code for the TCI is **649**. The international-operator telephone service is ✆ **115**. Local directory assistance is ✆ **118**.

To call a phone carrier in the U.S., dial **0**, then **1**, and then the number. You can make domestic and international calls using your credit card or prepaid phone cards, available in $5, $10, and $15 denominations—although rates for either are often as exorbitant as calling direct from your hotel room (you'll be charged more than $2 a minute, depending on the time of day—and many hotels even charge $1 and up for local calls). Public payphones accept prepaid phone cards only. You can buy these prepaid phone cards at a number of retail outlets and hotels, including Leeward Marina, Avis, and Club Med (Provo); Parrot Cay (Caicos Cays); the Middle Caicos Co-op; and the Poop Deck (Grand Turk). If you have a GSM cellphone with international roaming capacity, you can use that on the islands; a money-saving option is to buy or rent a cellphone in the TCI (see the "Calling Home" box, earlier in this chapter).

Time The islands are in the Eastern Standard Time zone, and daylight saving time is observed.

Tipping Hotels often add 10% to 15% to your bill automatically, to cover service. If individual staff members perform various services for you, it is customary to tip them something extra. If you go on an island tour, watersports charter, or beach excursion, it's always a good idea to tip your guide 10% to 20%, depending on the level of service you receive. In restaurants 15% is appropriate unless a service charge has already been added; if in doubt, ask. Tip taxi drivers 10% to 15%.

Water Government officials insist that the water in Turks & Caicos is safe to drink. Nonetheless, stick to bottled water, especially if you have a delicate stomach.

3

Where to Stay in Providenciales & the Caicos Islands

The growing preponderance of high-end boutique resorts in Provo means that consumers looking for a budget island getaway should reserve well in advance for the handful of moderately priced options or be on the lookout for package deals on hotel websites, online travel-booking sites such as Orbitz, Expedia, and Travelocity, or massive travel search engines like Mobissimo and Kayak. Check this guide's hotel reviews before you book, and see what other travelers have to say about TCI lodgings on Frommers.com message boards.

In contrast to what's available on Provo and Parrot Cay and Pine Cay (the two privately owned Caicos Cays islands with hotel resorts), moderately priced lodgings are currently the *only* option in the rest of the Caicos islands. Of course, with the construction of the Royal Reef and St. Charles resorts in North Caicos, and the Turks & Caicos Sporting Club in Ambergris Cay (South Caicos), high-end resorting is just over the horizon for the less-traveled islands.

Keep in mind that the government imposes a mandatory 10% hospitality tax and many resorts charge an additional service charge of 10% or more. Also note that during high season—and the Christmas holidays in particular—resorts have minimum-stay requirements. Hotels throughout the Turks & Caicos accept most major credit cards, except where noted.

Finally, as you can see when comparing winter and summer rack rates listed below, visiting Provo in the off season can be considerably more economical than a high-season winter vacation. Be sure to check each hotel's website for money-saving package deals any time of year.

For information on villa or apartment stays in Provo and the Caicos Islands, go to "Tips on Accommodations" in chapter 2.

Hotel School

Change has come fast and furious to TCI, and with it the business of hospitality, with resorts working hard to meet the exacting standards of a growing international clientele. Some businesses have responded by outsourcing staff from such faraway places as the Philippines and Bali. But the folks at the Grace Bay Club believe in developing staff locally, and as such have created a **Hotel School** to train TCI workers and eventually staff from other islands in the hospitality and tourism business. "I strongly believe in being able to hire locally," says Grace Bay Club General Manager Nikheel Advani. "It helps retain our feel and it's doing the right thing. We want to become the premier hotel school in the Caribbean—that is our vision for the school and the island." For more information about the school, go to www.gracebay club.com.

1 Providenciales

Provo's 19km (12-mile) Grace Bay is where the majority of the islands' resorts and hotels are situated. Provo's lodgings are an easy 10- to 15-minute taxi ride from the airport.

Note: Both **West Caicos** and **South Caicos** are seeing serious development action. On uninhabited West Caicos, the **Ritz-Carlton** is developing a high-end, low-impact hotel/villa/resort complex. In South Caicos, still largely a sleepy fishing community, the island of Ambergris Cay is being developed into the **Turks & Caicos Sporting Club** by the Greenbrier Resort.

GRACE BAY
VERY EXPENSIVE

Beaches Turks & Caicos Resort & Spa 🐾 (Kids) This Grace Bay megaresort remains a perennial favorite among families. And with a whopping 453 units and a $68-million expansion that includes an additional 168 family suites, a water park, and a 1,115-sq.-m (12,000-sq.-ft.) swimming pool in the new Italian Village set for completion in 2007, it's remarkable that it all chugs along as smoothly as it does. The grounds are beautifully maintained, guests (especially kids) seem deliriously happy and busy, and weddings are held on-site on an almost daily basis. It's a winning formula: Rooms

Where to Stay in Providenciales & the Caicos Cays

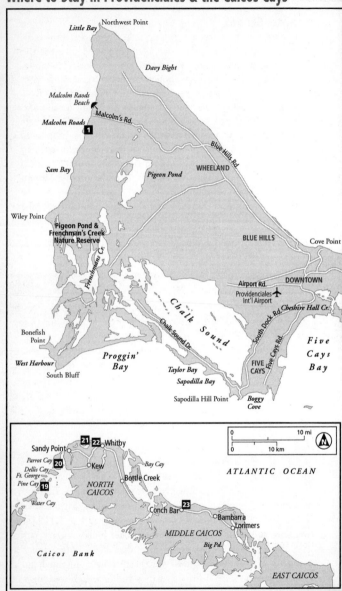

PROVIDENCIALES
Amanyara **1**
Beaches Turks & Caicos Resort & Spa **6**
Caribbean Paradise Inn **17**
Club Med Turkoise **15**
Comfort Suites **18**
Grace Bay Club **13**
Le Vele **11**
Miramar Resort **4**
The Palms **7**
Point Grace **10**
Ocean Club East **16**
Ocean Club West **12**
Queen Angel Resort **3**
Reef Residences/Coral Gardens **5**

Royal West Indies Resort **14**
The Sands at Grace Bay **9**
Sibonné Beach Hotel **8**
Turtle Cove Inn **2**

CAICOS CAYS
The Meridian Club **19**
Parrot Cay Resort **20**

NORTH CAICOS
Hollywood Beach Suites **21**
Pelican Beach Hotel **22**

MIDDLE CAICOS
Blue Horizon Resort **23**

⌒ *Tips* **Finding (Scarce) Convenient Stores**

For visitors who find they've forgotten an essential toiletry, crave a snack or a soft drink (and want to avoid paying through the nose for them in a resort restaurant or bar), or need an emergency ration of sunscreen or bug repellent, the Grace Bay area can be a tough place to locate such little conveniences—unlike in North America, where 7-Elevens and other convenience stores and grocery chains are just around the corner. There are virtually no vending machines around to pop in a few quarters and buy a candy bar or a sports drink, and the island has only one major grocery store, the Graceway IGA—and if you don't have a car, you'll have to take a taxi or the Gecko Shuttle to get there. Yes, many resorts are happy to provide a variety of toiletries, but a few well-placed convenience stores within walking distance of most resorts in and around Grace Bay supply the essentials and more—including beer, wine, and liquor, magazines and books, and local handicrafts. The following are open daily from around 9am to 6pm:

- **Norlani's** at the Reef Residences/Coral Gardens)
- **Norlani's** at the Sands on Grace Bay
- **Sandy's Convenience Store** at Ocean Club East
- **Neptune's Nectar** (in back of Ports of Call shopping village)

---

are nearly impossible to come by in high season without reservations made long in advance.

And yet, you wish the rooms were brighter, bigger, and warmer, and that deluxe suites were more, well, special—especially in comparison with similarly priced luxury suites elsewhere on Grace Bay. Yes, the older part of the resort is in the process of being refreshed (the decor is spiffier in the French Village, the newer section), and the rooms need it; some have a dark, slightly moldy feel and rattling air conditioners. You wish the food at the buffet looked more appetizing. You wish the resort's beach wasn't so tightly packed with people, vendors, beach floats, you name it—an anomaly on the luxuriously spread-out sands of Grace Bay.

This resort is part of the Sandals chain of all-inclusive hotels, though unlike most Sandals, families with kids are welcome here—and welcome here with a bang. The price tag is high, but the all-inclusive designation means you get plenty for your money: all your meals and drinks, excellent watersports, winning service from a huge staff of nearly 800 employees, a full-service nursery with cribs, swings, rockers, and a full coterie of nannies with whom you can leave babies and toddlers, even a spa, the **Red Lane** (open 8am–8pm daily). A Sesame Camp is available for kids 5 and under; actors dressed as characters from *Sesame Street*—Elmo and his friends Cookie Monster, Grover, and Zoe—are on hand to interact with small children. A Pirates Island Kids Club camp has daily activities for children 6 to 12. Gratuities are included for everything, so you don't have to worry about stuffing your pockets full of small bills and change and doling out tips all day. If you've got a gambling itch, 24-hour slot machines are available on the patio near the Turtles Bar. Note, however, that you'll pay extra for many spa treatments, certain scuba-diving courses and island excursions, and international telephone calls.

Accommodations come in 12 different "categories" and a variety of configurations and bedrooms. All rooms and suites have king-size beds. The higher-category suites have four-poster beds, a "Premium Bar" and fully stocked refrigerator based on your personal requests, and 8am-to-8pm concierge service. The luxury suites offer a really nifty amenity: 24-hour butler service, with professionally trained butlers catering to your every need. The largest unit, the French Village three-bedroom suite, can accommodate up to 11 people. Nightly entertainment—from movies to family game shows to adult discos—is held on the Main Stage in the French Village, so if you prefer to be away from the evening action, request a room elsewhere. And keep in mind that not all rooms and suites have ocean views; some have pool and/or garden views.

Food is available somewhere on the resort 24 hours a day, even though room service is offered only in the butler-suite categories (see above). Among the 10 restaurants, you can get Italian **(Giuseppe),** Tex-Mex **(Arizona's),** seafood **(Schooners),** or Asian **(Kimonos).** **Reflections** offers casual-fare buffets for breakfast, lunch, and dinner. For the kids, the very cool **Bobby D's** is a 1950s-style diner with typical kid faves like burgers, hot dogs, and spaghetti. The resort's showcase restaurant, **Sapodilla's,** is adults-only and features Continental cuisine; reservations are recommended.

Lower Bight Rd. (P.O. Box 186), Providenciales, Turks and Caicos, B.W.I. ⓒ **800/ 232-2437** in the U.S. or 649/946-8000. Fax 649/946-8001. www.beaches.com. 453 units. Prices based on 2 nights (minimum stay): Winter $420–$510 double, $640 1-bedroom suite, $1,200 2-bedroom suite for 4, $1,680 3-bedroom family suite; off season $385–$440 double, $575–$675 1-bedroom suite, $1,090 2-bedroom suite for 4, $1,525 3-bedroom family suite. Rates are all-inclusive. AE, DISC, MC, V. **Amenities:** 10 restaurants; 7 bars; 6 outdoor pools; golf course (nearby); 4 lit tennis courts; fitness center; spa; 2 saunas; kayaks; windsurfing; Hobie Cats; Aqua Trikes; snorkeling; volleyball; basketball; childrens center w/pool; game room; massage; nurses station; babysitting; laundry service; dry cleaning; Wi-Fi; Internet cafe (extra cost); nonsmoking rooms; 3 shops; rooms for those w/limited mobility. *In room:* A/C, ceiling fan, TV, dataport, fridge, coffeemaker, hair dryer, iron/ironing board, safe; CD players, in-room bars, and bathrobes available in concierge rooms.

Club Med Turkoise &

Set on 28 hectares (69 acres) of sun-blasted scrubland on a white strip of beachfront overlooking Grace Bay, this adults-only all-inclusive resort was one of the pioneers of Grace Bay when it opened in 1984. Today it remains an appealing oasis of charm and communal fun. Although Club Med Turkoise is more typical of the big, hyperactive Caribbean resorts than anything else on Grace Bay, it's one of the most casual Club Meds in the region.

The village-style cluster of basic two- and three-story accommodations contains colorful, newly renovated rooms with twin or king-size beds, all designed with beachfront living in mind.

Meals are included, as well as most drinks (except the real good stuff, like champagne, certain premium liquors and wines, and canned and bottled drinks; be sure to check the fine print before you book). Among the three restaurants, **La Mer** has grilled meats and is open in the evening only. Most meals are served at long communal tables. A dance club keeps residents active, if they wish, from 11:30pm to at least 3am nightly.

Grace Bay, Providenciales, Turks and Caicos, B.W.I. © **800/258-2633** in the U.S. or 649/946-5500. Fax 649/946-5497. www.clubmed.com. 297 units. Winter $1,545–$1,722 per person weekly; off season $1,300–$1,600 per person weekly. Rates include all meals, certain drinks, and most activities. AE, MC, V. No children under 18 allowed. **Amenities:** 3 restaurants; 2 bars; open-air nightclub; beach lounge; outdoor pool; 8 tennis courts (4 lit); gym; kayaking; sailing; snorkeling; windsurfing; softball; volleyball; basketball; flying trapeze; laundry service; coin-operated laundry; dry cleaning; Wi-Fi; nonsmoking rooms; shops. *In room:* A/C, TV, minifridge, coffeemaker, hair dryer, iron/ironing board, safe, clock radio/CD player.

Grace Bay Club &&&

This supremely comfortable boutique resort is one of the island's older hotels (opened in 1993) and remains one of its top lodgings, constantly reinventing and refreshing itself but staying true to its original commitment to excellence. The price is high, but if you can afford it, you'll get plenty of pampering and superb food for your money—and a whopping repeat business proves they're doing something right. It doesn't hurt that the resort sits on the largest oceanfront acreage on Grace Bay, property that more than doubled in length after the acquisition of additional footage in 2005. This coincided with a massive expansion that added 38 luxurious, family-friendly condos positioned within four low-density "villas," each set directly on the beach. (Like that of most other resorts on Grace Bay, the condos are privately owned but are available for guest bookings.) *Note:* The original 22-suite adults-only hotel is currently closed for renovations but was scheduled to open in early 2007.

The resort structures have a sun-burnished Mediterranean look and feel. Each of the villa accommodations has an eclectic kind of elegance, with travertine-tile floors, custom-made imported furnishings, deep private patios, and magnificent oceanfront views. Suites (except junior suites) and penthouses each have their own state-of-the-art kitchens (granite countertops, stainless-steel appliances), washing machines, and dryers. Four 446-sq.-m (4,800-sq.-ft.) penthouses have oceanfront showers and outdoor Jacuzzis, among other luxuries. Suites contain dining tables that can seat 12, and an increasingly popular trend, particularly during the Christmas holidays, is to hire one of the resort chefs to cook a private in-suite dinner (starting at $120 per person).

The hotel's main restaurant, **Anacaona** (p. 88), is Provo's top dining choice—but it remains adults-only. As part of the new expansion, the kid-friendly **Grill** offers casual alfresco dining with grilled seafood, paninis, salads, and a kids' menu. The beachfront **Lounge,** with its Hamptons-style white-cushion seating and glowing fire pit, is one of the best spots on island to have a cocktail and watch the sunset on Grace Bay. A new program called Kids Town offers a full menu of kid-friendly eco-activities and half- or full-day excursions.

Grace Bay Rd. (P.O. Box 128), Providenciales, Turks and Caicos, B.W.I. © **800/946-5757** in the U.S. or 649/946-5050. Fax 649/946-5758. www.gracebayclub.com. 60 units. Winter $725 junior suite, $865–$1,095 1-bedroom suite, $1,295–$1,495 2-bedroom suite, $1,995 3-bedroom suite, $5,000–$7,000 penthouse; off season $425–$555 junior suite, $525–$825 1-bedroom suite, $865–$1,245 2-bedroom suite, $1,195–$1,495 3-bedroom suite, $3,000–$5,525 penthouse. Rates include continental breakfast, round-trip airport transfers, and transportation anywhere in the Grace Bay area. MAP (breakfast and dinner) $70 per person extra. AE, MC, V. **Amenities:** 2 restaurants; 2 bars; 2 outdoor pools; 2 lit tennis courts; fitness center; 465-sq.-m (5,000-sq.-ft.) spa; Jacuzzi; car rental; business services; room service (7am–9pm daily); massage; laundry service; high tea (3:30–4:30pm); boating excursions; deep-sea fishing; kayaks; sailing; windsurfing; bikes. *In room:* A/C, TV w/DVD/CD player, Wi-Fi, kitchen (excluding junior suites), hair dryer, safe, bathrobes, ceiling fan, washer/dryer (excluding junior suites).

The Palms ☆☆☆ This $85-million boutique resort, which opened in early 2005, has already established itself as one of Grace Bay's classiest resorts, with some of the most beautifully appointed rooms on the island. But don't let its cool good looks intimidate you. Yes, it has a chichi South Beach–style pool scene and Provo's only croquet lawn, and the neo-Palladian centerpiece of the resort is referred to as the Mansion (fashioned after the classic Caribbean estates designed by Oliver Messel, the late British theatrical decorator who also created Princess Margaret's "cottage" in Mustique)—but beneath that frostily elegant facade is a casual, congenial Turks & Caicos vibe and even kid-friendly amenities, such as the Conch Kritters Club, a daily activities program for kids 4 to 12 that might include lizard hunting, beach Olympics, or kite flying.

Although The Palms offers a few conventional, albeit well-decorated and large double rooms (popular in the off season), the majority (72) of its units are one-, two-, and three-bedroom suites, equally divided among five separate coral-stone buildings that form a horseshoe-shaped curve encompassing a grand view of the beach. The so-called mansion is home to a clubby wood-paneled bar and the resort's main restaurant, **Parallel23,** which serves what it calls "tropical fusion" cuisine from an open kitchen with a wood-burning oven; the restaurant's outdoor terrace fronts Palm Place, with shops on either side of a palm-lined courtyard. **Plunge,** the pool bar and restaurant, has a sunken dining terrace and a swim-up bar—as you lie around the serpentine infinity pool, you can check your e-mail with the complimentary Wi-Fi and drink a toast to another tough day at the beach. The 2,323-sq.-m (25,000-sq.-ft.) Spa at the Palms features white tented cabanas limned by a reflecting pool.

White and bright define the interiors: Accommodations are big, airy, and stylish, featuring custom-made mahogany furniture, white linens in meltingly soft Egyptian cotton, beachy wainscoting, and white and off-white color tones—the Hamptons meets colonial Africa. Bathrooms are luxurious retreats clad in elegant marble with large hydro-massage tubs and power showers. Five spectacular 279-sq.-m (3,000-sq.-ft.) penthouses feature three bedrooms, big, windowed kitchens, and travertine terraces with indoor and outdoor showers and sweeping Grace Bay views.

Grace Bay Rd. (P.O. Box 681), Providenciales, Turks and Caicos, B.W.I. © **866/877-7256** or 649/946-8666. Christmas holiday reservations: © **305/532-7900** or e-mail (info@thepalmstc.com) only. Fax 649/946-5502. 72 units. www.thepalmstc.com. Winter $575–$750 double, $1,200–$3,150 suite, $3,950–$5,300 penthouse; off season $300–$400 double, $650–$1,375 suite, $2,750–$3,750 penthouse.

Note: Double rooms and 1-bedroom suites are not available for reservation during the Christmas holidays. Children under 12 stay free in parent's room. Rates include full buffet breakfast and round-trip airport transfers. AE, MC, V. **Amenities:** 2 restaurants; conventional bar; pool bar; infinity pool; fitness center (personal trainers available on request); full-service spa; Jacuzzi; sauna; yoga, Pilates, and meditation studio; 18-hole golf course (5 min. away); tennis courts; croquet lawn; nonmotorized watersports equipment and kids' beach toys; salon (men's barbershop in the works); 24-hr. room service; babysitting/nanny service; Wi-Fi; 5 shops; Conch Kritters Club (cost extra). *In room:* A/C, TV (flat-panel LCD TVs in penthouses), high-speed Internet, full kitchens w/Viking appliances (suites and penthouses), minibar, hair dryer, safe, ceiling fan; daily butler services in penthouses.

Point Grace 👑👑👑 This boutique hotel, one of the most charming and atmospheric on the island, opened in 2000 on one of the best beaches in the entire Western Hemisphere, a lyrical crescent of sand ringed by turquoise sea. Point Grace has racked up one award after another since it opened, including a 2005 World Travel Award for the Caribbean's Leading Boutique Hotel, and in a short time has perfected an almost effortless grace. The motif is vintage West Indies, and the services and amenities are first-rate, ranging from twice-daily maid service to midday sorbets on the beach. You can request to be met at the airport in a Rolls-Royce, have a private in-room chef prepare your meal, or have a picnic hamper readied for island excursions. The **Thalasso Spa at Point Grace** (open daily 9am–6pm) is a full-service on-site spa that offers treatments using sea mud and seaweed, among other delicacies.

The complex features exceptionally spacious one-, two-, three-, and four-bedroom suites and penthouses, furnished with Indonesian hardwood and teak and brightened by crisp white Frette linens and African artwork. Hand-painted tile and mahogany grace the bedrooms, and each suite has a beautifully appointed kitchen.

Point Grace is set in the Princess Alexandra National Park, a protected marine reserve on the north coast. The hotel is named for Grace Hutchings, who spent her honeymoon here in a small cottage more than a century ago. Four replicas of Grace's original honeymoon cottage surround a pretty pool and courtyard. On-site is the excellent restaurant **Grace's Cottage** (p. 89), perhaps the most romantic spot to dine in the TCI.

Grace Bay (P.O. Box 158), Providenciales, Turks and Caicos, B.W.I. © **866/924-7223** in the U.S. or 649/946-5096. Fax 649/946-5097. www.pointgrace.com. 28 units. Winter $595–$935 double, $1,140–$2,730 2-bedroom suite, $1,445–$1,705 3-bedroom suite, $2,730 4-bedroom suite, $4,800–$6,800 penthouse; off season $425–$750 double, $695–$2,185 2-bedroom suite, $1,015–$1,365 3-bedroom suite, $1,765–$2,185 4-bedroom suite, $4,200–$6,000 penthouse. MAP meal plan (lunch and dinner, exclusive of drinks) $87 per person per day. Rates include continental buffet breakfast, complimentary house cocktails and hors d'oeuvres at the pool bar 5–6pm, and round-trip airport transfers. AE, DISC, MC, V. **Amenities:** 2 restaurants; 2 bars; outdoor pool; golf (nearby); oceanfront spa; concierge services; limited room service; babysitting; business center w/high-speed Internet; nonsmoking rooms; bikes; kayaks; library; sailing. *In room:* A/C, TV, dataport, kitchen, minibar, hair dryer, iron, safe, bathrobes, beverage maker, washer/dryer.

EXPENSIVE

Le Vele 𝔊 *Value*   This classy addition to Grace Bay is a bastion of sleek elegance on a picture-perfect stretch of beach. The boutique resort contains only 22 units but is a great option for families. Each of the one-, two-, and three-bedroom condominium suites has room to spare, with oceanfront views, wraparound balconies, and full kitchens (excluding the studio suites). If you're looking for a quiet, intimate spot with a clean, spacious design steps away from the sea, this should fit the bill. Although it doesn't have a restaurant or bar, you're minutes away from a number of fine Grace Bay options. You can also use the hotel's nightly Dining Shuttle to get to restaurants that aren't close by. Or you can take advantage of the suites' complete kitchens, with ovens, ranges, microwaves, stainless-steel fridges, and dishwashers. This is good value for Grace Bay, with its prime location and self-catering facilities (see "Shopping for Self-Catering," in chapter 4).

Grace Bay, Providenciales, Turks and Caicos, B.W.I. ⓒ **888/272-4406** or 649/941-8800. www.levele.tc. 22 units. Winter $413 double, $578 1-bedroom suite, $825 2-bedroom suite, $1,183 3-bedroom suite; off season $303 double, $413 1-bedroom suite, $605 2-bedroom suite, $908 3-bedroom suite. Extra person $60 per night. Rates include continental breakfast delivered to your suite and round-trip airport transfers. AE, DISC, MC, V. **Amenities:** "Vanishing edge" pool; fitness center; shopping shuttle; nightly dining shuttle; concierge/excursion desk; babysitting; bikes; computer facilities; DVD library; Wi-Fi. *In room:* A/C, TV, high-speed Internet access, full kitchens (studio suites have kitchenettes w/fridge, microwave, utensils, china, and glassware), hair dryer, safe, Jacuzzi, washer/dryers (excluding studio suites).

Ocean Club Resorts 𝔊 *Kids*   These two condo-hotel complexes are within a mile of one another, both with prime oceanfront acreage on Grace Bay. The original, **Ocean Club East,** lies across from the Provo Golf Club, spread across a 3-hectare (7½-acre) piece of landscaped property. It shares amenities with its newer sister resort, **Ocean Club West,** and a complimentary shuttle runs between the two. Both comprise a low-lying series of buildings surrounding gardens and a courtyard.

Both resorts have 86 suites, among them studio suites, junior suites, and one-, two-, or three-bedroom deluxe suites—many with ocean views and fully equipped kitchens (studios have kitchenettes only). (The main difference between East and West is that only Ocean Club East offers studio deluxe and one-bedroom beachfront suites.) Except for the studio suites (the cheapest rental), accommodations are spacious and comfortable, with large screened balconies. The decor is light, bright, and pleasant if not particularly exciting— but on a slice of beach this delicious, who's spending much time in the room?

With their large suite size and fully appointed kitchens, these resorts are family-vacation favorites. Both resorts have a Kids Clubhouse, a day camp for children 3½ and up from 9:30am to 1pm daily.

Ocean Club East's **Gecko Grille,** in the Ocean Club Plaza, is a popular Provo restaurant for Continental dining. Also in the plaza is an annex for Art Pickering's Provo Turtle Divers Ltd. (see "Scuba Diving & Snorkeling," in chapter 5), as well as a shop that sells good local artwork, Art Provo (p. 117). There's also a daily shuttle-bus service for dining in the evenings and a part-time shuttle bus for daytime shopping, both for a small fee.

Grace Bay Beach (P.O. Box 240), Providenciales, Turks and Caicos, B.W.I. © **800/ 457-8787** in the U.S. or 649/946-5880. Fax 649/946-5845. www.oceanclubresorts. com. 186 units. Winter $240–$295 studio suite, $399 junior suite, $435–$545 1-bedroom suite, $595–$705 2-bedroom suite, $835–$910 3-bedroom suite; off season $180–$225 studio suite, $275 junior suite, $315–$335 1-bedroom suite, $415–$485 2-bedroom suite, $550–$600 3-bedroom suite. Call about Christmas holiday rates. Children under 12 stay free in parent's room. AE, DISC, MC, V. **Amenities:** 3 restaurants (Seaside Café is in Ocean Club West); 3 bars; 3 freshwater pools; golf; 3 lighted tennis courts; fitness room; sauna; watersports; kids' programs; meeting rooms; high-speed Internet; concierge; babysitting; bikes; convenience store; dive shop; fishing. *In room:* A/C, TV/VCR, dataport, kitchen (kitchenettes in studios), hair dryer, safe, ceiling fan, washer/dryer (excluding studios).

Reef Residences/Coral Gardens ✿ Big changes are coming to this popular Grace Bay resort, which fronts one of the beach's top snorkeling and diving spots on Bight Reef in the Princess Alexandra National Park. Coral Gardens is undergoing a $6-million renovation that includes the addition of 24 new garden suites known as the Reef Residences at Coral Gardens, a new pool, a new gourmet restaurant (the **Epicurean**) serving Italian-style cuisine, and a greatly expanded spa and fitness center. The popular restaurant Coyaba is moving to what is currently patio space at the Caribbean Paradise Inn (see below). In its place will be the expanded spa, with more treatment rooms and state-of-the-art fitness facilities. The current resort suites will be refreshed, a good thing: In spite of their supremely generous space (full kitchens and even walk-in closets in some!) and deep, expansive balconies, at press time the suites were looking a little worse for wear, with motel-quality linens and slightly beat-up bathrooms. The new expansion should also help open up the resort and make the public spaces feel less cramped. What hasn't changed is the excellent snorkeling and diving opportunities literally right out your door; the on-site dive operator **Cactus Voyager** offers scuba courses, snorkeling tours, and complimentary snorkeling equipment. The new restaurant, the Epicurean, is expected to open in late 2006—but you can always rely on the **Beach Café** for tasty food at breakfast, lunch, and dinner and the delicious feel of sand in your toes while you're dining. Ask about the Tuesday-evening **Tide Affair** five-course dinner—a barefoot gourmet extravaganza served right on the beach ($60 per person; reservation only).

An all-inclusive option includes such amenities as all meals, beverages in designated areas, a daily spa treatment, and the complimentary use of a car for your entire stay.

P.O. Box 281, Grace Bay, Providenciales, Turks and Caicos, B.W.I. ℂ **800/532-8536** in the U.S. or 649/941-3713. Fax 649/941-5171. www.coralgardens.com. 30 units. Summer $285–$495 1-bedroom suite, $550–$615 2-bedroom suite, $860 3-bedroom suite, $585–$685 penthouse; call about winter 2007 rates. Extra person 10 years or older $60 a night. Children under 10 stay free in parent's room. Rates include full breakfast and round-trip airport transfers. AE, DISC, MC, V. **Amenities:** 2 restaurants; 2 bars; 2 outdoor pools; golf (nearby); spa; fitness center; excursion desk; 24-hr. room service; babysitting; nonsmoking rooms; bikes; convenience store; dive and snorkel shop; fishing; kayaks; sailing; scuba diving; snorkeling; Wi-Fi. *In room:* A/C, TV, dataport, full kitchen, hair dryer, iron, safe, bathrobes, beverage maker, CD and DVD players, washer/dryer (in penthouses and Ocean Grand suites).

Royal West Indies Resort ℛ

This is one of the most reliable, well-managed condo-hotel resorts along Grace Bay, offering family-friendly lodging and a prime location on one of the best sections of beach, between the Grandview on Grace Bay and Club Med. Surrounding the property are well-manicured gardens, the centerpiece of which is a 24m-long (79-ft.) pool set against a backdrop of tropical fruit trees. Guests have a choice of oceanfront, oceanview, studio, or garden-view one- and two-bedroom suites. Suites are large and have balconies or patios and good-size kitchenettes. Two-bedroom suites can be subdivided into one-bedroom accommodations or self-sufficient units. The interiors are furnished in typical resort fashion—don't expect 400-thread-count linens or designer toiletries, but don't expect standard chain-motel decor either—the rooms have sturdy, well-maintained furnishings and are perfectly comfortable. The ladies at the front desk can be sort of starchy, but everything else works beautifully. Even if you're not a guest, I strongly recommend a meal at **Mango Reef** (www.mangoreef.com), the casual poolside restaurant with consistently fresh, tasty food.

Grace Bay (P.O. Box 482), Providenciales, Turks and Caicos, B.W.I. © **800/332-4203** in the U.S. or 649/946-5004. Fax 649/946-5008. www.royalwestindies.com. 99 units. Winter $235–$375 studio, $340–$540 1-bedroom suite, $490–$720 2-bedroom suite; off season $175–$275 studio, $255–$410 1-bedroom suite, $360–$495 2-bedroom suite. Extra person 13 or over $35 per night. Rates include round-trip airport transfers. AE, MC, V. **Amenities:** Restaurant; bar; 2 outdoor pools; golf (nearby); Jacuzzi; babysitting; bikes; kayaks; sailing; scuba diving; snorkeling; Wi-Fi. *In room:* A/C, TV, kitchen, hair dryer, iron, safe, ceiling fan, washer/dryers.

The Sands at Grace Bay 🏝 This sprawling all-suites condominium resort is another popular, well-managed family choice, set on a particularly lovely stretch of Grace Bay Beach, between Sibonné and Point Grace. Low-lying buildings flank manicured gardens and pools. Choose from studio, one-bedroom, two-bedroom, or three-bedroom suites—each of which is fully appointed, with sunny resort furnishings and screened terraces. The suites also have full kitchens (studios have kitchenettes) and washer/dryers—great for family stays. The Sands has two other very winning amenities: Spa Tropique, an on-site spa with state-of-the-art treatments (open daily 9am–7pm), and one of the beach's most popular restaurants, **Hemingway's on the Beach** (p. 93).

Grace Bay, Providenciales, Turks and Caicos, B.W.I. © **877/777-2637** in the U.S. or 649/946-5199. Fax 649/946-5198. www.thesandstc.com. 116 units. Winter $250–$500 studios, $375–$750 1-bedroom suites, $475–$775 2-bedroom suites, $725–$1,150 3-bedroom suites; off season $175–$325 studios, $300–$500 1-bedroom suites, $350–$525 2-bedroom suites, $475–$750 3-bedroom suites. Extra person $25. Maximum of 2 children under 12 stay free in parent's suite. Rates include round-trip airport transfers. AE, DISC, MC, V. **Amenities:** Restaurant; bar; 3 outdoor pools; tennis court; spa services; fitness center; Jacuzzi; nonmotorized watersports equipment; tour desk; babysitting; dry cleaning; bikes; conference room; convenience store; dive shop. *In room:* A/C, TV, dataport, full kitchens (kitchenettes in studios), hair dryer, iron, safe, bathrobes, ceiling fan, washer/dryer.

MODERATE

Caribbean Paradise Inn *Value* This intimate, cozy inn is a real find, just minutes away from Grace Bay Beach, visible from the balconies of the second-floor rooms. Two stories of rooms overlook the pool and a lovely tropical courtyard. Combination bedroom and living area, with a patio or balcony, the rooms are in the process of being upgraded and refreshed. The small bathrooms have showers only. The inn features one family-friendly suite, with a separate living room and kitchenette. Jean Luc Bohic is the personable owner. Late-breaking news: Chef Paul Newman is moving the popular restaurant **Coyaba** from its longtime location at Reef Residences/ Coral Gardens to the bar/patio area here; it should open by October 2007.

Grace Bay (P.O. Box 673), Providenciales, Turks and Caicos, B.W.I. ℂ **877/946-5020** in the U.S. or 649/946-5020. Fax 649/946-5022. www.paradise.tc. 16 units. Winter $155–$215 double, $195–$290 suite; off season $120–$140 double, $155 suite. Extra person $35; children under 5 stay free in parent's room. Rates include buffet breakfast. MC, V. **Amenities:** Bar; outdoor freshwater pool; watersports; babysitting; laundry service. *In room:* A/C, TV, dataport, minibar/fridge, hair dryer, safe, beverage maker, ceiling fan.

Comfort Suites   This is the first franchise hotel to open on Provo. As a Comfort Suites hotel, it is far superior to the standard format, and the hospitality provided by the staff is exceptional. The handsomely landscaped property lies across the road from Grace Bay Beach and is within an easy walk of many attractions, including the casino. Guests stay here in one of the spacious junior suites, with either a king-size or two double beds, or else in one of the so-called honeymoon suites (you don't have to be a honeymooner to book one of these). Accommodations are spread across two three-floor structures, enveloping an Olympic-size swimming pool and a courtyard.

Grace Bay, Providenciales, Turks and Caicos, B.W.I. ℂ **888/678-3483** in the U.S. or 649/946-8888. Fax 649/946-5444. www.comfortsuitestci.com. 100 units. Winter $150–$160 double, $170 suite; off season $135–$150 double, $160 suite. Rates include breakfast. Children under 16 stay free in parent's room. Extra person $35. AE, DISC, MC, V. **Amenities:** Bar; outdoor pool; babysitting; nonsmoking rooms. *In room:* A/C, TV, dataport, fridge, hair dryer, iron, safe, beverage maker.

Miramar Resort *(Value)*   This well-priced option, formerly the Erebus Inn, has a unique location atop a hill overlooking Turtle Cove Marina. The panoramic views of the turquoise sea and the gentle curve of Grace Bay are a rare treat in this generally flat landscape. But accommodations can be iffy. The room we were given was spacious and clean, but I found it a little depressing, smelling of heavy-duty cleaning supplies and outfitted in furnishings that never rise above motel chic (the website features some nice-looking rooms that looked nothing like ours). On the positive side, the Miramar has a big pool, and on-site is a highly regarded restaurant, **Magnolia Wine Bar & Restaurant** (p. 96). On the negative side, the pool is located in a sea of concrete and the restaurant takes pains to note that it is not affiliated with the resort. Still, if you don't plan to spend substantial time in your room or want to be close to the Turtle Cove marina, Miramar is certainly a money-saving option in pricey Provo.

Grace Bay (P.O. Box 238), Providenciales, Turks and Caicos, B.W.I. ℭ **649/946-4249.** Fax 649/946-47044. www.miramarresort.tc. 19 units. Winter $135–$145 oceanview double, $120–$130 pool-view double; off season $135 oceanview double, $120 pool-view double. Extra person $30. MC, V. **Amenities:** Restaurant; bar; outdoor pool; 2 clay tennis courts; fitness center; nonsmoking rooms; Internet kiosk. *In room:* A/C, TV, dataport, fridge, hair dryer, electric kettles.

Sibonné Beach Hotel ✯ (Value)   This was one of the first hotels constructed on the fabulous sands of Grace Bay Beach. The hotel is a fantastic value and has charm to spare, but don't expect anything grand or a huge laundry list of resort amenities. What it does have is a laid-back, informal vibe, alluring courtyard gardens, and knock-out Grace Bay views. It's considerably more personable than any chain-style hotel, with rooms that have a light, breezy decor and a serious emphasis on comfort—everything has been nicely updated. For a stupendous deal on Grace Bay, book the one-bedroom upstairs apartment, detached from the actual hotel. It has a full kitchen (with pots, pans, plates, the works), a separate living room, a big, comfortable bed, and two oceanfront patios, one screened, one open—you'll feel as if you have your own sunny beachfront cottage within spitting distance of the million-dollar sands of The Palms. On-site is the **Bay Bistro** (p. 90), a sunny beachside restaurant offering barefoot diners breakfast, lunch, and dinner.

Grace Bay (P.O. Box 144), Providenciales, Turks and Caicos, B.W.I. ℭ **800/528-1905** in the U.S. or 649/946-5547. Fax 649/946-5770. www.sibonne.com. 29 units. Winter $125–$260 double, $350–$395 apt; off season $99–$185 double, $275 apt. AE, MC, V. **Amenities:** Restaurant; bar; outdoor pool; babysitting; laundry service. *In room:* A/C, TV, dataport, fridge, hair dryer, iron, safe, beverage maker, ceiling fan.

NORTHWEST POINT

Those in the know say that this section of Provo represents the future of the country's hospitality industry. Unlike Grace Bay's long, developable stretch of beach, the beaches at the Northwest Point are serendipitous little coves with pockets of powdery white sand and turquoise seas. As the area develops, the plan is to create lots of green-belted area and ensure no structure over three stories tall is built. The waters along the Northwest Point are part of the **Northwest Point Marine National Park,** a protected 8km-long (5-mile) reef system that features some of the world's top wall and reef diving.

Currently the Northwest Point has only two accommodations: Amanyara (see below), and the **Northwest Point Resort** condominium hotel (www.northwestpointresort.com). To reach either, you travel through the delightful Blue Hills neighborhood. Make time to stop at one of the beachfront shacks to enjoy supremely fresh conch dishes, good music, and a sunny barefoot vibe (see "Dining Da Blue Hills," in chapter 4).

Amanyara 🏆🏆🏆 *(Kids)*   The first Amanresorts property in the West Indies was such a big deal when it finally opened in early 2006 that *Travel & Leisure* magazine devoted an entire cover article to it. It's a big deal, all right, bringing a whole new style of luxury to the region. It's a luxe that's the polar opposite of fussy and ostentatious, however, with Amanresorts' trademark elegant simplicity of form, integrity of materials, and devotion to eco principles. Yes, the prices are exorbitant but with a refreshingly grown-up transparency of costs; included in the rates are just about everything in the mini-bar—which includes some high-end goodies like chocolate-covered graham crackers, dark chocolate, and macaroons—all outgoing calls, and wireless Internet service, unlike at other hotels where the final bill fairly sags under the weight of all the little extras.

The 40 individual pavilions are private, stand-alone houses, three sides of which are glass. Outside, wraparound patios are enveloped in native scrub brush, sea grape, and sea ox-eye daisies. It feels a bit like sleeping in a treehouse, except you're rooted to the ground in any number of elemental ways. You won't see riotous resort colors turned loose here: Earth tones and monochromes rule. Walls are crafted of imported hardwoods, and the terrazzo floor is streaked with teak inlays. Bathrooms have solid sisal mats and waterfall showers. A pebbly path leads from the pavilion through the brush to the sea; lizards sun themselves on the patio. It's all very earthy by day, but when evening comes you're in James Bond territory: With the flick of a switch, the curtains on all sides discreetly descend, smoothly and silently screening out the native world. Flip open your laptop and go online, groove to the surround-sound Bose system, or switch on the flatscreen TV. Or simply open the louvered screens and let in the sweet night air.

Amanyara is much more than just the rooms, however wonderful. The pavilion motif continues in the classically aligned main resort buildings, which practically float on reflecting pools and ponds, in obeisance to Amanresorts' love of all things symmetrical. The bar has a golden imported-wood ceiling that soars toward the sunlight. The lovely infinity pool, with a speckled black Indonesian lava (nonskid) surface, has three linen-wrapped sofa-bed pods—everywhere you look, in fact, are more cushiony sofas to plop yourself into, many with eye-level views of the sunset horizon. Sunset at Amanyara, in fact, has already become a mandatory activity for locals.

Dining options include the **Restaurant,** which serves an Asian-influenced international cuisine either inside or on a candlelit alfresco patio, and the **Beach Club,** which serves lunch in a beachside setting, has an alfresco patio. You can also get a light lunch on the bar terrace. The resort is very kid-friendly; management is happy to provide not only cribs and nannies but diapers, Diaper Genies, and even homemade baby food.

Currently, three-bedroom villas with full kitchens are being constructed and will be available for rent.

Northwest Point, Providenciales, Turks and Caicos, B.W.I. ℂ **866/941-8133** or 649/941-8133. Fax 649/941-8132. www.amanyara.net. 40 private pavilions. Winter $1,650–$1,980; off season $1,350–$1,650. AE, MC, V. **Amenities:** 2 restaurants; bar/lounge; outdoor pool; 2 clay tennis courts; fitness center; spa; nonmotorized watersports; babysitting; laundry service; boutique shop; library; Wi-Fi. *In room:* A/C, flatscreen TV, minibar/fridge, hair dryer, iron/ironing board, safe, Bose sound system, Wi-Fi.

TURTLE COVE

At press time there was more resort activity at the Turtle Cove Marina. The **Queen Angel Resort,** a 56-condo hotel, opened in June 2006. All rooms and suites have full kitchens; the resort plans to open a restaurant and bar and a disco (ℂ **649/941-7907;** fax 649/941-7908; opening special rates of $175 per night).

In the development stages is the **Third Turtle Club** (www.third turtleclub.com), a luxury condo-hotel resort with a secluded beach and marina. It's being built on the spot where the Third Turtle Inn, the first hotel on the island, formerly stood.

Turtle Cove Inn 🄰 *Value*   This two-story hotel, built in a U shape around a freshwater swimming pool amid tropical vegetation, is a favorite with divers and boaters. It's a fine choice for vacationers on a budget (it's the well-run sister inn to Sibonné, the charming and equally well-run Grace Bay oceanfront resort). A few feet away, boats dock directly at the hotel's pier, which juts into Seller's Pond amid the many yachts floating at anchor. Each bedroom is simply but comfortably furnished, with views over either the pool or the marina. The on-site **Aqua Bar & Terrace Restaurant** is a popular Turtle Cove hang, serving tasty Caribbean cuisine, fresh seafood, and Saturday-night sushi.

Turtle Cove Marina, Suzie Turn Rd. (P.O. Box 131), Providenciales, Turks and Caicos, B.W.I. ℂ **800/887-0477** in the U.S. or 649/946-4203. Fax 649/946-4141. www. turtlecoveinn.com. 28 units. Winter $105–$140 double, $180 marina-view apt; off season $85–$120 double, $155 marina-view apt. Children 12 and under stay free in parent's room. AE, MC, V. **Amenities:** Restaurant; bar; outdoor pool; scooter and bike rental; car rental; babysitting; laundry service. *In room:* A/C, TV, dataport, fridge, safe, ceiling fan.

2 Caicos Cays

PARROT CAY

Parrot Cay Resort 𝒢𝒢𝒢   This laid-back luxury resort, a favorite of celebrities and honeymooners, lies on an isolated and very private 400-hectare (988-acre) island with a powdery white-sand beach. The compound features 10 white "modern colonial"–style buildings, each with a terra-cotta tile roof. Rooms have louvered doors that open onto terraces or verandas, oyster-white walls with tongue-and-groove paneling, terra-cotta floor tiling, and mosquito netting artfully draped over four-poster beds. The large tiled bathrooms are beautifully appointed with a big tub and a shower and the spa's Invigorate toiletries. The best rooms by far are the beach houses and villas, which offer utter privacy and direct access to the beach. Beach houses have plunge pools and hardwood verandas; beach villas are even bigger, with swimming pools and kitchenettes.

Many come to Parrot Cay primarily for the sublime treatments in the **COMO Shambhala** holistic spa, hands down the finest spa in the Caribbean, which recently expanded to encompass a 613-sq.-m (6,600-sq.-ft.) space wrapped in a sea of glass that looks out over the island wetlands. Inside several free-standing wooden pavilions are treatment salons where Eastern-influenced healing and rejuvenating therapies are applied by Balinese healers. The spa has both a yoga studio and a Pilates studio, as well as a new outdoor Jacuzzi garden outside the women's locker room. The spa's wonderfully clean-smelling Invigorate products (also in the resort bathrooms and sold in the resort shop) are addictive. In addition, the resort has an infinity pool and access to scuba diving, Hobie Cats, snorkeling, kayaks, and water-skiing.

The two restaurants both offer two different menus: an elegant Mediterranean cuisine and a healthful Shambhala spa menu, which uses organic foods. Breakfast and dinner are served inside the main building at the **Terrace.** Lunch and dinner are served in **Lotus,** a torch-lit poolside restaurant where diners can discreetly ogle celebrities in the dim candlelight or simply drink in the ultraromantic surrounds.

Parrot Cay (P.O. Box 164), Providenciales, Turks and Caicos, B.W.I. © **877/754-0726** in the U.S. or 649/946-7788. Fax 649/946-7789. http://parrotcay.como.bz. 60 units. Winter $680–$865 double, $1,580 1-bedroom suite, from $2,220 1-bedroom beach house, $2,670–$4,890 beach villa; off season $450–$700 double, $1,075–$1,270 1-bedroom suite, $1,640–$1,780 1-bedroom beach house, $2,105–$3,895 beach villa. Rates include full American breakfast and round-trip airport transfers by car and hotel boat. Packages available on website. AE, MC, V. Reached by a 30-min. private boat ride north from Provo, leaving from Leeward Marina. **Amenities:** 2 restaurants; 2 bars; outdoor pool; 2 tennis courts; spa; fitness center; Jacuzzi; sauna; excursion desk; library/game room w/high-speed Internet; limited room service; babysitting; laundry service; nonsmoking rooms; boutique; fishing; kayaks; nature trail; snorkeling. *In room:* A/C, TV/DVD, dataport, kitchenette (in some), minibar, hair dryer, safe, beverage maker, ceiling fan, radio/CD player.

PINE CAY

The Meridian Club 🐠🐠   Don't expect luxury of the marble-floors or gilded-chandeliers variety—this is what is lovingly referred to as "barefoot elegance"—and be prepared to live without television, radio, and even air-conditioning. This is the high life of an entirely different sort, the kind where you and a lucky few others are securely ensconced on a private island paradise. The Meridian Club is one of the TCI pioneers, having been established on 324-hectare (800-acre) Pine Cay way back in 1973. To get here, you either take a 30-minute boat ride from Leeward Marina or fly in to the tiny island airstrip used by Meridian Club guests and the island's home-owners. The island has no cars: To get around, you either hoof it or, if you're in a hurry, tool around in an electric golf cart. The beach in front of the resort is simply extraordinary, and sand dollars float up without fail on the tawny sands of Sand Dollar Point, mere yards away. The snorkeling in the coral gardens offshore is satisfyingly good. The meals—included in the rates—are hearty, nutritious, plentiful, and insanely tasty—like good home-cooked food, which it basically is. The rooms have spacious bathrooms, a screened-in porch, and outdoor patios with decadent outdoor showers. If you require still more privacy, opt for the Sand Dollar Cottage, a six-sided "hut" with a flagstone floor and lots of light from the louvered windows, set apart from the other rooms and almost directly on the beach.

It's all wonderful, with one minor complaint: The decor in the rooms and dining area is a tad stale and dated. Perhaps this is something the new management team—which includes Butch Clare, former chairman of the TCI Tourist Board, and the folks from the Royal West Indies resort in Provo—will address in the coming months. Check the resort website for the latest packages and special offers. ***Note:*** Children under 12 are only allowed as guests in the months of May and June.

Pine Cay, Providenciales, Turks and Caicos, B.W.I. © **866/746-3229** or 781/828-0492. E-mail reservations to reservations@meridianclub.com. www.meridianclub.com. 12 units. Winter $795–$895 club rooms, add $100 per night for the Sand Dollar Cottage; off season $550–$650 club room, add $100 per night for the Sand Dollar Cottage. Rates include all meals, afternoon tea, and round-trip airport transfers by car and hotel boat. Extra person $150 per night. No credit cards (cash, traveler's checks, or personal checks acceptable). Closed Aug 1–Oct 31. Reached by a 30-min. private boat ride north from Provo, leaving from Leeward Marina. **Amenities:** Restaurant; bar; outdoor pool; tennis court; spa services; laundry service; nonsmoking rooms; bikes; board games; boat excursions; computer room w/high-speed Internet; fishing; golf cart rentals; kayaks; shop; snorkeling; telephone booth. *In room:* Hair dryer, safe, ceiling fan.

3 North Caicos

Rural, green, and charmingly slow-paced, North Caicos has its share of gorgeous powdery-sand beaches, which at press time you could enjoy with a few other lucky souls during stays at modest, moderately priced lodgings. Construction is underway, however, for two major new luxury hospitality enterprises: **Royal Reef Resorts** (www.royalreefresort.com), on heretofore uninhabited Sandy Point, and the **St. Charles** resort condominiums (www.stcharlestci.com) on Horsestable Beach.

Hollywood Beach Suites   This is a real getaway and almost feels like camping out, except you have a fully equipped suite in which to park your bones, and a kitchen (and outdoor barbecue grill) to cook the day's catch (supplied by local fishermen if you request it in advance). You can also have a local cook prepare a real island meal for you; just ask the helpful manager. Bikes, kayaks, and snorkeling equipment are available for guest use, but you may be tempted to spend your time simply daydreaming in a hammock on the lovely beach (or on the deck overlooking the water) just steps away from the suites.

Hollywood Beach Dr., Whitby, North Caicos, Turks and Caicos, B.W.I. © **800/551-2256** in the U.S. or 649/231-1020. Fax 702/973-6659. www.hollywoodbeachsuites.com. 4 units. Winter $356 1-bedroom suite; off season $253 1-bedroom suite. Rates include round-trip taxi pickup/drop-off. AE, MC, V. **Amenities:** Bikes; board games; grill; kayaks; snorkeling equipment. *In room:* A/C, TV/DVD/VCR, dataport, fully equipped kitchens, hair dryer, iron/ironing board, ceiling fan, washer/dryer, no phones.

Pelican Beach Hotel   This small, pleasant guesthouse feels as if it's from another era, with a pitched timbered ceiling and wood paneling; the only thing missing is the ticking of a grandfather clock. Outside, casuarina pines shade a conch-strewn beach lapped by turquoise seas. Owners Clifford and Susie Gardiner call this place the "unresort" and have created a mellow homey vibe, which Susie's delicious home cooking only serves to underscore. The rooms are plain but comfortable. You can snorkel nearby, have the Gardiners arrange a boat excursion or island tour, or join the bird-watchers who flock here to see pink flamingos and ospreys. Or relax and enjoy the peace and quiet. As they like to say here at Pelican Beach: "Sometimes, you'll find, doing nothing is wonderful."

Pelican Beach, North Caicos, Turks and Caicos, B.W.I. (*) 649/946-7112. www.pelican beach.tc. 16 units. Winter $225 double with meals, $145 double without meals; off season $160 double with meals, $119 double without meals. Rates include full breakfast and dinner daily and round-trip taxi pickup/drop-off. DISC, MC, V. **Amenities:** Restaurant; bar service; bikes. *In room:* A/C, fridge.

4 Middle Caicos

The largest island in the TCI is also the least populated, and hotel/motel-type lodgings—not to mention restaurants, grocery stores, and shops—are currently almost nonexistent. Many visitors stay in rented villas. For a selection of villas, go to www.tcimall.tc/middlecaicos.

Tip: Don't forget to bring mosquito repellent, especially if you plan to visit some of the Middle Caicos Lucayan caves.

Blue Horizon Resort *✦*   This small resort with self-catering cottages enjoys one of the islands' most breathtaking locations, high on a green bluff overlooking the coral-sand swimming beach of Dragon Cay Cove and the blue-green waters of Mudjin Harbor. The resort is comprised of blue-tile-roofed cottages and villas dotting the hillside. The accommodations are modest, but the views from the cottage windows and patios are superb. All of the cottages have kitchens, and Blue Horizon will arrange to have your groceries delivered to your cottage if you provide them with your grocery list 2 weeks before your arrival; you can buy fresh-caught fish and lobster from local fishermen once you arrive. *Note:* The inn was up for sale at press time, so do call ahead to make sure it's still a viable operating lodging.

Middle Caicos Island, Turks and Caicos, B.W.I. (*) 649/946-6141. Fax 649/946-6139. http://bhresort.com. 28 units. $185–$275 daily; $1,250–$1,850 weekly. MC, V. **Amenities:** Snorkeling. *In room:* A/C (in some), TV, kitchen, washer/dryer (in some).

4

Where to Dine on Providenciales & the Caicos Islands

You will eat very well in Provo—the quality and freshness of the food, much of it imported, is remarkable—but *you will pay big-city prices to do so.* That may be why so many resorts and hotels offer full kitchens and other self-catering facilities, to help offset the daily pain of paying for double-digit-entree meals. Know, too, that economical fast-food restaurants and chain eateries are nonexistent here (for the time being, at least). Luckily, most resorts offer complimentary breakfasts, either full American style or Continental, and you can get a good slice of pizza or a burger for a reasonable price in a number of venues. And even luckier still, many celebrated home cooks (on less-traveled islands) will prepare traditional island meals for visitors.

You can sample cuisines from around the world here, from Italian to Asian to Mexican. You will dine on dishes that have melded Continental-style cuisine with Caribbean influences. But what will you eat that actually *comes from* the Turks & Caicos? Like many

---

Tips Buying Spirits

Liquor, liqueurs, wine, and beer are sold at liquor stores, grocery stores, and convenience stores (see "Shopping for Self-Catering," below, for a few store locations and contact information), but no alcohol is sold in these venues on Sunday. Liquor by the drink, wine, and beer are available 7 days a week in restaurants and bars. While you're on the islands, be sure to try the local beer, **Turk's Head,** produced in a microbrewery in Providenciales. It comes in a light, delicious lager, and a heavier amber. *Note:* Legal drinking age is 18 on the islands.

Shopping for Self-Catering

Staying in Provo and have a full kitchen at your fingertips? Stock it with the following self-catering options. Get your meats, produce, snacks, and kitchen staples at the **Graceway IGA** (© **649/941-5000**; www.gracewayiga.com) on Leeward Highway (which also sells beer, wine, and liquor, but not on Sun—you can only get alcohol in restaurants and bars on Sun). Buy fresh fish straight off the **Leeward Marina docks;** arrive at 5 or 6pm when the boats come in. Or head to **LTC Fisheries** (© **649/941/7358**) in Five Cays. For liquor, beer, and wine, go to the **Wine & Spirits Liquor Store** (© **649/941-8047**) in the Saltmills shopping center, the **Tipsy Turtle** in Turtle Cove Marina, or the **Wine Cellar** (© **649/946-4536**) on Leeward Highway—you can also buy soft drinks and water at liquor stores. (Be sure to try the local Turk's Head beer, available in lager or amber.) You can buy prepared foods (like dinner entrees, appetizers, or savory meat pies), hard-to-find exotic ingredients, and gourmet groceries at **Gourmet Goods** (© **649/941-4141**), in Grace Bay Court on Grace Bay Road. Gourmet Goods will also prepare and serve complete catered dinners in your villa or condo.

other Caribbean islands, the TCI grows little of its own food and must import much of its foodstuffs to meet the demands of an international tourist clientele. Local hydroponic farms provide restaurants with fresh lettuces, cucumbers, tomatoes, and herbs. The true bounty comes from the sea, in the form of fresh conch, Caribbean lobster (but only in season, Aug–Mar), and glorious fish in all sizes and flavors.

By all means, look for restaurants that serve local specialties, like the charming beach shacks that dot the Blue Hills (see "Dining Da Blue Hills," later in this chapter), where you can sample such local dishes as rice and peas; curry goat, fish, and chicken; oxtail stew; all things conch (conch fritters, conch chowder, and conch seviche); all things lobster (in season); hominy grits; and banana bread. If you want to experience a good sampling of the local cuisine, get your hands on a copy of the *Turks and Caicos Islands Food* cookbook (see "Turks & Caicos Islands Cookbook" sidebar, later in this chapter).

Keep in mind that the government adds a 10% tax on all restaurant bills. A few restaurants will add a service or gratuity charge, particularly for tables of six or more people. Always check your bill before tipping to make sure a gratuity has not already been figured in to the total.

Currently, Providenciales and the Caicos Islands are not late-night dining destinations. Most restaurants stop serving around 10pm and close down altogether by 11pm.

1 Providenciales

Most of the dining choices in Provo are found in the Grace Bay area. Provo has two other good dining neighborhoods in Turtle Cove and the Blue Hills; see listings below plus the "Dining Da Blue Hills" box later in this chapter.

If you don't have a car and the restaurant is not within walking distance, you can have your hotel call a taxi for you, or you can take the **Gecko Shuttle** (www.thegecko.tc) from your hotel to the restaurant and back again. The shuttle stops at practically every restaurant in the Grace Bay area. In high season the Gecko runs every 30 minutes from 10am to 11pm Sunday through Wednesday and 10am to 2am Thursday through Saturday. Buy shuttle passes or tokens at your resort or hotel. For more information on the shuttle and a map of the shuttle stops, go to "Getting Around the Turks & Caicos Islands," in chapter 2.

BLUE HILLS

Da Conch Shack *ⓡⓡ* CONCH/CARIBBEAN Formerly Bugaloos (and moved to a location closer to downtown), this is the happiest place in town. It's set outside in an open white shack literally set in the sand on a rise above the Blue Hills Beach. Steps away is the RumBar, separated by more sand and white picnic tables. As Bugaloos, this was a conch institution beloved by locals and visitors alike, and it hasn't missed a beat in its new incarnation as Da Conch Shack. Down below, in the shallow aquamarine reef waters, small conch pens hold live conch, refreshed daily by fishermen. On the beach the conch is drawn out of its shell, beaten, and then served any number of ways, whether as superb conch fritters or what may be the island's best conch chowder—tomatoey, full of vegetables, and with just the right pinch of spice. Conch this fresh is a revelation—and the cooks know just how to prepare it so that it's not rubbery or tough. Take

Dining Out on an Evening Pass

Even if you're not staying there, you can sample the food at **Beaches Turks & Caicos Resort & Spa** (p. 110) by purchasing an evening pass. For $140 per adult ($70 per child), you can enjoy all the food and drink you want from 6pm to 2:30am. Just keep in mind that two of the restaurants, **Kimonos** (Japanese steakhouse) and **Sapodilla's** (the resort's signature white-glove restaurant serving international cuisine), require advance reservations (and they book up quickly). Also keep in mind that Sapodilla's is an adults-only eatery. Prefer to eat breakfast and dinner and make a day of it at Beaches? Purchase a day pass for $120 adults ($60 per child), and from 9am to 5pm you can partake in the numerous all-inclusive watersports and other activities—an especially fun option for the kids in your party. For more information, call ✆ **649/946-8000.**

off your shoes, press your face to the sun, sip the suds off a Turk's Head lager, and join in the laid-back merriment.

Blue Hills. ✆ **649/946-8877.** No reservations. Conch dishes $10–$12. No credit cards. Daily noon–late.

DOWNTOWN

Hole in the Wall ⟨ JAMAICAN/CARIBBEAN   This popular local hang on Old Airport Road has some of the best island food on Provo. It's so good at preparing conch that it won the 2005 Conch Festival grand prize for the best overall conch dishes and best conch chowder—no mean feat in this conch-obsessed restaurant environment. You can get real island food here, from very good jerk chicken or pork to fried fish, curry goat, and barbecued ribs. Sides include peas 'n rice and fried plantains. Breakfast is the real island deal, with seasoned codfish, cornmeal porridge, peas 'n grits, and johnnycakes. Hole in the Wall even offers free pickup/drop-off service to and from Grace Bay accommodations.

Downtown at Williams Plaza, Old Airport Rd. ✆ **649/941-4136.** No reservations. Main courses $11–$14. No credit cards. Daily 8am–late.

GRACE BAY

Note: At press time the French-Mediterranean restaurant **Coco Bistro,** on Grace Bay Road, had been sold to new owners. Please call

Where to Dine in Providenciales & the Caicos Cays

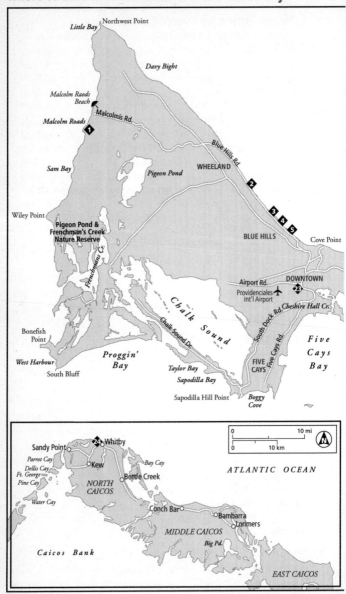

ATLANTIC

OCEAN

Water Cay

Little Water Cay · Donna Cut

Donna Cay

Emerald Point

Mangrove Cay

LEEWARD

Crist Point

Grace Bight

Forbes Point

Grace Bay

Stubbs Cove

Long Bay Beach

Sirus Cove

Long Point

Long Bay

TURTLE COVE

Lower Bight Rd.

KINGSTON

LONG BAY HILLS

RICHMOND HILLS

THE BIGHT

Juba Point Salina

Caicos Bank

Turtle L.

Flamingo L.

Bristol Hill Rd.

Turtle Tail

Juba Point

Cooper Jack Point

PROVIDENCIALES
Anacona **15**
Aqua Bar & Terrace **7**
Baci Ristorante **6**
Banana Boat Restaurant **6**
Bay Bistro **12**
Beach Café **9**
Beaches Turks & Caicos
  Resort restaurants **10**
Bella Luna **20**
Caicos Café **17**
Coyaba Restaurant **18**
Da Conch Shack **5**
Fairways Bar & Grill **17**
Gecko Grille **16**

Grace's Cottage **14**
Hemingway's on the Beach **13**
Hey Jose's Cantina **22**
Hole in the Wall **23**
Magnolia Wine Bar &
  Restaurant **8**
Matsuri Sushi Bar **21**
Parallel23 **11**
The Restaurant at Amanyara **1**
Sailing Paradise **3**
Smokey's on Da Bay **4**
Three Queens **2**

NORTH CAICOS
Pelican Beach Hotel **24**

in advance (© **649/946-5369**) to get the latest information regarding this popular spot.

VERY EXPENSIVE

Anacaona 🐚🐚🐚   MEDITERRANEAN/CARIBBEAN   Set beneath thatched-roof palapas and the starry evening sky alongside the Grace Bay Club, this is the top dining option in Provo. Among its winning attributes is an unbeatable location directly facing the Grace Bay Beach, which it shares with the hotel's hip and happening alfresco Lounge, where you can enjoy a frothy drink before dinner. As the sun sets, the atmosphere becomes more romantic, with flickering light from the free-standing torches and candlelight on the tables. Chef Eric Brunel has a remarkably deft touch with fish—whether sautéed, seared, or grilled, Brunel's fish is never overcooked or oversauced. Equally good are the rare ahi tuna on a bed of spinach and the seared red snapper served with tapenade. A highly recommended starter is the Providenciales bouillabaisse, brimming with wahoo, shrimp, and scallops plus a splash of rum. And the chocolate tasting platter finale is overkill in the best possible way. Anacaona offers an extensive wine list. Kids under 12 are not allowed.

In the Grace Bay Club, Grace Bay Rd. © **649/946-5050.** Reservations recommended. No children under 12. Lunch salads, sandwiches, and platters $10–$21; dinner main courses $28–$33. AE, MC, V. Daily noon–4pm and 7–11pm.

Celebrating the Conch

The Caribbean queen conch may be endangered elsewhere, but here in the Turks & Caicos, it's plentiful and a tasty staple for the creation of many dishes, whether served raw, fried, curried, or even jerked. For a sampling of all things conch and a real taste of Blue Hills hospitality, it's hard to beat the **Turks & Caicos Conch Festival,** held the last Saturday in November. Local restaurants vie to win top honors for best conch concoctions, including conch chowder, conch curry, and conch salad, to name a few of the contested dishes. In 2005 the Best in Festival honor was awarded to the downtown eatery Hole in the Wall (p. 85), and Beaches Resort won the prizes for Best Conch Specialty (jerked conch) and Best Conch Salad. Just in its third year, the conch festival has become a popular celebration, with music, food, conch-blowing, and a great Blue Hills Beach location. For more information, go to **www. conchfestival.com.**

Coyaba Restaurant && CONTINENTAL/CARIBBEAN

Note: At press time this popular gourmet restaurant was moving from its longtime spot in Reef Residences Coral Gardens to the patio/bar area of the Caribbean Paradise Inn; it is expected to open by October 2007.

Chef Paul Newman (no, not that one) shows off his culinary flair in preparing some of the island's freshest and best seafood. His island dishes show a strong European influence. Start your meal with tempura shrimp in Barcelo honey–rum sauce or the Blooming Jerk (onion with a garlicky clementine-and-papaya-seed aioli). The Turks & Caicos conch and seafood chowder is also delicious. For a main course, try one of the many good fish dishes—pan-fried grouper in a buttery caper vinaigrette, perhaps, or oven-baked mahimahi prepared tandoori-style. The Caribbean spiny lobster is served here as a rich thermidor, updated with a Dijon-and-mushroom crème. For dessert, nothing tops the apple pie accompanied by Blue Mountain coffee from Jamaica. Ask about Chef Newman's tasting menu and chef's table, for up to 10 people. Service here is usually top-notch but was a little off the last time I visited—I hope it was just a one-time glitch.

Next to the Caribbean Paradise Inn, Grace Bay. © 649/946-5186. Reservations required. Main courses $22–$39. AE, MC, V. Wed–Mon 6–10pm.

Grace's Cottage &&& CARIBBEAN/CONTINENTAL This

beautifully romantic spot only seats 62 people, and you can bet the majority of them are couples holding hands across the candlelit tables. Grace's Cottage is a little architectural gem: a warm buttery-yellow cottage with Victorian-style gingerbread trim and lattice-work. You dine on the cottage terrace or on one of the patios surrounding the cottage, nestled in tropical vegetation and softly illuminated lighting. Inside you can enjoy an aperitif at the mahogany bar before taking a chair at one of the teak tables covered with Egyptian cotton tablecloths. The food is as exceptional as the setting: Chef Alberto Artiles prepares seafood in light, sophisticated ways, but he also has a way with duck, lamb, and beef. A grilled beef tenderloin was requested rare, and it was brought to the table cooked to order, beautifully finished with a Madeira reduction. If it's on the menu, begin with the flavorful Providenciales bouillabaisse. For a main course you might sample pan-fried island strawberry grouper, Caribbean jerk encrusted Chilean sea bass, or (in season)

West Caicos lobster capriccioso. Desserts are delicious and include a state-of-the-art chocolate soufflé or blueberry cherry cheesecake.

In the Point Grace Hotel, Grace Bay. ℂ 649/946-5096. Reservations required. Main courses $23–$38. AE, MC, V. Daily 6:30–10:30pm.

Parallel23 ⋪⋪ TROPICAL FUSION/INTERNATIONAL Try if you can to snag a table on the restaurant terrace. It's an elegant setting, overlooking Palms Place courtyard and situated in the Mansion, The Palms resort's homage to vintage Caribbean estates. Otherwise, you'll be perfectly comfortable ensconced in the off-white interior, with views of the open kitchen and colorful artwork on the walls. Chef Jasper Schneider has serious fish-cooking creds: He worked with Eric Ripert at Azur at Le Bernardin in the La Quinta Resort & Club, and Ripert knows a little bit about preparing seafood. Chef Schneider has created a menu here at The Palms that boldly dips into cuisines from around the world. The menu's East/West conceit combines disparate ingredients in very clever ways; a roast chicken, for example, is paired with Caribbean plantains and a hearty sancocho (meat) broth. Pork chops come roasted with chipotle onions and black-bean stew. The Bar at Parallel23 has the kind of overstuffed sofas and dark-grain wood you'd find in an old-time gentleman's club in some colonial outpost—it's small but supremely comfortable and welcoming.

In The Palms resort, Grace Bay. ℂ **649/946-8666**. Reservations required. Main courses $24–$75. AE, MC, V. Daily 8–11am, noon–3pm, and 6–10pm.

EXPENSIVE
Bay Bistro ⋪ CARIBBEAN/EUROPEAN The location is fantastic, directly on Grace Bay Beach fronting Sibonné hotel. You'll practically be kissed by salt air and sea spray as you dine. In fact, you can enter from the beach, along a wooden plank in your bare feet. The food is hearty and good, with a menu developed by Clive Whent, the same chef who cooks at the Aqua Bar & Terrace (in Sibonné's sister lodging, the Turtle Cove Inn). It features a good assortment of standard Caribbean specialties (conch fingers, fish wrap, snapper, tuna, and mahimahi), steak, chicken, and rack of lamb. The blackened-shrimp salad is a tasty starter for dinner and makes a filling lunch. The Bay Bistro serves food almost all day long, from hearty breakfasts to lunch and dinner; have a drink at Junior's Bar before dinner.

In the Sibonné hotel, on Grace Bay. ℂ **649/946-5396**. Reservations recommended. Main courses $22–$32; lunch $10–$12. AE, MC, V. Daily 7am–10pm.

Bella Luna ✦ ITALIAN   Situated up in "the glass house" on a slight rise along Grace Bay Road, Bella Luna provides yet another of Provo's many atmospheric dining experiences. The food ain't bad, either. Chef Cosimo Tipodi gives his Italian menu a few subtle Caribbean tweaks. You can start with beef carpaccio or conch frittelle, grilled conch patties with a jerk mayo sauce. Veal and chicken are served a number of classic Italian ways. Pastas are recommended, particularly seafood pastas like the linguine tuttomare, with fresh lobster (in season only) and shrimp with your choice of sauce: in a marinara, cream, or rosé sauce. Linguine marechiaro is basically linguine in clam sauce with a kicky spiciness. Weekday lunch is served here in high season only.

Grace Bay Rd., Grace Bay. ✆ 649/946-5214. Reservations recommended. Main courses $22–$38. AE, MC, V. Mon–Fri 12:30–2:30pm (in high season only); daily 6:30–10pm.

Caicos Café ✦✦ CARIBBEAN/FRENCH   This is one of those irresistible places that gets under your skin; it's a favorite among locals, but visitors also find the warm, romantic ambience and consistently delicious food hard to resist. It's set on the terrace deck of what appears to be a Caribbean cottage with gingerbread trim, gaily illuminated with strings of twinkling lights and flaming torches. Colorful Haitian artwork blankets the walls. The menu, written on a blackboard, is extensive and reflects the French/Mediterranean influences of its chef/owner Pierrik Marziou. But the vibe is pure Turks & Caicos, laid-back and happy, with a leisurely what-me-worry? approach to dining and life in general. Fresh seafood is a big draw; I loved the seafood gumbo, spiced just right. People around me were raving about the buttery shrimp risotto, and conch figures heavily on the menu—the conch chowder is a meal in itself. Fresh breads and desserts are baked in the cafe's own bakery.

Caicos Café Plaza, Grace Bay Rd. ✆ 649/946-5278. Reservations recommended. Main courses $24–$33. MC, V. Tues–Sat noon–3pm; Mon–Sat 5–11pm.

Gecko Grille INTERNATIONAL   This brightly decorated, popular spot in Ocean Club Plaza in the original Ocean Club Resort (East) has a range of foods that runs the culinary gamut from Italian (pastas, caprese salads, bruschetta) to all-American (steaks, chops, surf and turf) to Caribbean (plantain-crusted grouper, coconut-crusted mahimahi, Caribbean lobster tail). The outdoor terrace is a very pleasant place on which to dine. The Gecko Grille bar lounge also offers 75 different premium vodkas.

Dining Da Blue Hills

The welcoming beach shack bar/restaurants along the Reef Harbor shoreline of northwest Provo represent what one local describes as a "taste of old-time Provo." For a therapeutic immersion in the TCI art of studied languor, you can't beat a meal at one of the shacks in Provo's oldest settlement along the rural Blue Hills road, dotted with pastel-painted churches and schools. In fact, many visitors come here straight from the airport, kicking off their cold-weather armor and city-slicker shoes to dig their toes in the warm sand, stare out at the sun-dappled azure seas, and dine on conch freshly pulled from the sea. Even better, the food at these shacks is as fresh and soul-satisfying as anything you'll find in Provo. Probably the most popular Blue Hills shack is **Da Conch Shack** (formerly Bugaloos, but moved to a location closer to downtown), where live conch is held in pens in the shallows below and brought up to order (see review, earlier in this chapter). Another popular spot is the brightly colored **Sailing Paradise** (✆ **649/946-5885**), where you dine on beachside decks on fresh cracked conch and fried fish. **Smokey's on Da Bay** (✆ **649/241-4343**) serves barbecued ribs and has a Wednesday-night fish fry. Farther down the road toward Northwest Point is the oldest of the Blue Hills restaurants, **Three Queens** (✆ **649/941-5984**), a favorite local hangout, especially on Friday nights. The classically trained chef wears a white toque and gives island classics (like oxtail stew, which he braises in red wine) tender loving culinary treatment. Hours for all the Blue Hills shacks vary, so call before you go, but the general opening times are Monday to Saturday from 11am until past sunset. Bring cash.

Ocean Club Plaza, Grace Bay Rd. ✆ 649/946-5880. Reservations recommended. Main courses $23–$46. AE, MC, V. Tues–Sun 6–10pm.

Matsuri Sushi Bar ✿ SUSHI/JAPANESE   Sushi lovers swear by the sushi served at this island outpost, next to the Graceway IGA. You can get set dinners of sushi, sashimi, rolls, or combos. A number of rolls are available, from standard California to spicy octopus.

This may be one of the few places in the sushi world where you can get a conch maki.

101 Graceway House (next to the Graceway IGA), Leeward Hwy. © 649/941-3274. Main courses $25–$29; sushi rolls $5–$15. DISC, MC, V. Mon–Sat noon–3pm and 6–10pm.

MODERATE

Beach Café ℛ CARIBBEAN   This very modest beachside restaurant is literally on the beach—you can take off your flip-flops and feel the sand between your toes while you eat. It's one of those perennially reliable spots that leave you satisfied and happy. It's open virtually all day and is the perfect spot to recharge after snorkeling the Bight Reef, just steps away. At breakfast the mango pancakes are a hit (and you need those carbs to soldier on in your quest for a tan). Lunch flows into dinner, with the same menu and prices, and you can't go wrong with the Guyanese pepper-pot soup with callaloo (local spinach), Janet's Fish Tea (seafood in a curry broth with vegetables and Chinese noodles), or a homemade Trinidadian rôti: flatbread stuffed with curried chicken, vegetables, or seafood—as good as any I've every had. Kids' meals include burgers and hot dogs.

In Reef Residences Coral Gardens, Grace Bay. © 649/941-5706. Reservations recommended. Main courses $9–$23. AE, MC, V. Daily 8–11am and 11:30am–9:30pm.

Fairways Bar & Grill *Finds* CARIBBEAN/CONTINENTAL   With all the ocean-side/oceanfront/oceanview dining available in Provo, why oh why would you want to dine on a golf course? Well, if you could find one this pleasingly atmospheric and solid, you needn't ask. In fact, you can eat here all day if you really want—the restaurant is open from 7am to 3pm and then from 6 to 10pm, and in between the bar serves such hearty snacks as conch fritters, popcorn chicken, and burgers. The bright, airy, high-ceilinged space has French doors that open onto an outdoor patio with seating overlooking the golf course greens. The menu is extensive; choose from salmon, pork chops, lamb chops, rare blackened tuna loin (with spicy mango chutney), steak, or pasta. A kids' menu offers burgers, chicken fingers, and cheese sandwiches.

Provo Golf & Country Club, Grace Bay Rd. © 649/946-5833. Reservations requested. Main courses $24–$39. AE, MC, V. Daily 7am–3pm; Mon–Sat 6–10pm.

Hemingway's on the Beach ℛ CARIBBEAN/INTERNATIONAL   This casual place is jumping morning to night, and the ocean-side location is only half the enticement. With a setting like this, the food doesn't have to be this good—but it is, and hallelujah. The coconut shrimp was as light as a feather—well, let's just say it was fried to perfection, not heavy or greasy in the least. If lobster is in season, order it here, simply and elegantly grilled. Hemingway's is also a fine lunch choice, serving a terrific mango shrimp salad over Provo lettuce with mango chutney, a very respectable hamburger, and good chicken and chips: marinated and fried Caribbean jerk chicken breast with the restaurant's signature seasoned fries. The service is attentive but relaxed and friendly. At night torches and candlelight heighten the romantic ambience. A bell sits on a pole on the upper deck of the restaurant, there to ring if anyone spots JoJo the dolphin cruising the Grace Bay waters; see "Spotting JoJo the Dolphin," on p. 109.

At The Sands at Grace Bay. ℂ 649/941-8408. Reservations required. Main courses $15–$42. AE, MC, V. Daily 8am–10pm.

INEXPENSIVE

Hey José's Cantina MEXICAN/PIZZA/AMERICAN   One of the focal points of a small shopping center in the center of the island, this lighthearted place is run by Gary and Marilyn Walter. Here you can enjoy the best margaritas in Provo. The parade of burritos, tacos, quesadillas, chimichangas, and grilled steaks and chicken will make you think you've been transplanted to some fiery little eatery along the Tex-Mex border. Also popular, especially with expatriate North Americans who have had their fill of grouper and cracked conch, are the richly topped pizzas. Available in three sizes, they culminate with a variety known as the Famous "Kitchen Sink," with virtually everything you can think of thrown into the mix.

Central Sq., Leeward Hwy. ℂ 649/946-4812. Pizzas $7–$16; main courses $7.95–$22. MC, V. Mon–Sat noon–11:30pm (bar until midnight).

At press time the new **Restaurant at Amanyara** was accepting non–resort guests. The menu features Asian-infused international cuisine and is served either indoors or on a terrace overlooking the water at Northwest Point. I highly recommend arriving early so you can have a drink on the bar terrace and watch the sun go down. Dinner reservations are a must; please call ℂ 649/941-8133, and try to reserve a table well in advance.

TURTLE COVE

Aqua Bar & Terrace ℱ SEAFOOD/CARIBBEAN   Divers, boaters, and couples flock to this convivial dockside restaurant at

---

Island Scoop: Locally Made Ice Cream

For a sugary frozen treat and a break from the island heat, try one of the locally made ice creams and sorbets at **Island Scoop**. Fill a cone with traditional flavors such as chocolate or peach or try something a little more exotic like white mint or coffee 'n cookies. You can also get a range of shakes, smoothies, sundaes, and cookies. You'll find two Provo locations: Grace Bay Plaza (℡ **649/242-8511**) and on Dolphin Rd., next to Ports of Call (℡ **649/243-5051**). Northwest Point

---

Turtle Cove Marina, which is open for breakfast, lunch, and dinner. The setting, an enclosed outdoor bar and terrace overlooking the marina, packs 'em in. Nightly and weekly dinner specials are offered. Chef Clive Whent's classic home-smoked conch is served carpaccio-style with a wasabi-laced mayonnaise, or go for the extrarare coffee-rubbed tuna. The best of the signature dishes include blackened local lobster (in season only) served with a Thai coconut sauce or the pecan-encrusted conch with a spicy orange-butter sauce.

Breakfast is for creative types who prefer to build their own omelets or even their own bagels (here you can top yours with such hearty all-American sides as sausage, bacon, or cheddar cheese). If all this sounds like an early-morning grease overload, Aqua offers a tropical fruit plate served with waves of yogurt. At lunch you can sample a classic burger, fish or conch fingers, or Aqua's Clubhouse, with blackened chicken.

In the Turtle Cove Inn, Suzie Turn Rd., North Shore. ℡ 649/946-4763. Reservations recommended for dinner. Main courses $19–$32. AE, MC, V. Daily 7am–10pm.

Baci Ristorante ☂ ITALIAN   This spot enjoys one of the loveliest waterside settings in Provo, on the docks of the Turtle Cove Marina. Lacy iron doors lead out to terraced outdoor seating overlooking the water. The tasty cuisine, the romantic patio, the stone floors and wrought iron, and the whirling *Casablanca*-style overhead fans conspire to make this an agreeable stopover. (And admit it: It's also a nice break from all that conch.) Veal is served four different ways: in lemon butter sauce, in a red-wine peppercorn sauce, in a Marsala-and-mushroom sauce, or baked and topped with tomato sauce and mozzarella. The hearty pasta dishes include the usual suspects, such as fettuccine Alfredo and penne alla vodka (here with chicken). Baci also has kid-friendly brick-oven pizza, with plenty of toppings to choose from.

Turtle Cove Marina, Harbour Towne. (C) **649/941-3044**. Reservations recommended. Main courses $16–$27 (lobster in season commands market prices); lunch $10–$18. AE, MC, V. Daily noon–2:30pm and 6–10pm.

Banana Boat Restaurant CARIBBEAN/SEAFOOD   The Banana Boat is not the best restaurant on the island, but it's certainly one of the most convivial—there's not a yachtie on Provo who hasn't moored here to enjoy an island meal and a potent tropical drink. For a main course, you might try T-bone steak, cracked conch, or some freshly caught local fish. At lunch, favorites include lobster salad or a half-pound burger. No one in the kitchen fusses too much with these dishes, and here that's a good thing: Expect fresh and flavorful food. A choice seat is on the timber-and-plank veranda that juts out over piers on Turtle Cove.

Turtle Cove Marina. (C) **649/941-5706**. Main courses $13–$40 (surf and turf); lunch $6.50–$15. AE, MC, V. Daily 11am–11pm.

Magnolia Wine Bar & Restaurant *&&* MEDITERRANEAN/ ASIAN/INTERNATIONAL   You won't find a setting like this one anywhere else on the flat scrublands of Provo: high on a hill overlooking Turtle Cove Marina, with the sparkling lights of the island spread out before you. You could almost be dining in a cliff-side trattoria overlooking the Mediterranean Sea. Magnolia has only been around since 2002 but has already established itself as one of

---

Turks & Caicos Islands Cookbook

If you want to take home treasured recipes from serious Turks & Caicos Islands cooks, both professional and celebrated local home cooks, look for a copy of the *Turks and Caicos Islands Food* cookbook, a colorful hardcover published in 2005 by the Turks and Caicos Islands Red Cross ($20; proceeds go to support the Red Cross). Among the recipes are Love's Fried Fish with Tamarind Sauce, from Isadora Emanuel (Love), who runs Love's Restaurant in South Caicos; island jerk encrusted Chilean sea bass, from executive chef Alberto Artiles at Grace's Cottage in the Point Grace resort; and Pat's Dreamy Coleslaw, from Pat Simmons of Pat's Place in Salt Cay. You can buy the cookbook through the Red Cross or at various resorts throughout the islands and in the Unicorn Bookstore on Leeward Highway in Provo.

the best places to dine in Provo—both for the romantic outdoor setting and the delicious food. The chef has a sure hand when it comes to marrying flavors, and the sesame-seed-and-cracked-pepper-crusted rare seared tuna is emblematic of this approach. Nothing could be earthier or more flavorful than the bacon-wrapped pork tenderloin. Start with a Magnolia appetizer sampler (for two people), which features chicken spring roll, tuna tartare, tempura shrimp, and curried mussels.

At the Miramar Resort, Turtle Cove Marina. © **649/941-5108.** Reservations recommended. Main courses $24–$33. AE, MC, V. Tues–Sun 6–10pm; wine bar opens at 5pm.

2 North & Middle Caicos

Currently, there are few restaurant choices in North or Middle Caicos. **Pelican Beach Hotel** (© **649/946-7112**), in North Caicos, serves homemade meals, prepared by the owner, Susie Gardiner, but you must call ahead to reserve a table. Middle Caicos has largely self-catering options, although a small restaurant at the airport offers a few local specialties. Big changes are coming to the islands, so more dining options should be available soon.

5

Exploring Providenciales & the Caicos Islands

Most of the country's celebrated sports and activities revolve around, unsurprisingly, its ubiquitous resource: all that crystal-clear water with the mesmerizing emerald hue. Try scuba diving the spectacular underwater walls just offshore, fishing the coral reef or deep-water drop-offs, or leisurely exploring the little uninhabited cays and coves that dot the watery landscape.

Of course, there are plenty of nonwatersports-related things to do here, including golf, tennis, horseback riding, exploring historical attractions, caving, shopping, and enjoying state-of-the-art spa treatments. This chapter tells you how to explore the best the islands have to offer.

1 Beaches

It's no hype: The beaches of the Turks & Caicos are some of the most beautiful on the planet, thanks in large part to one of the few remaining unspoiled coral reef ecosystems in the Caribbean—or the world for that matter. This, the third-largest coral reef system on the planet, helps act as a breakwater against ocean surges for these islands, keeping the coastal waters calm and clear. It makes its presence known on land as well: Coral is literally the soft white sand beneath your feet.

The Caicos Islands have some of the country's best beaches, including world-class Grace Bay—and on many of them, yours will be the only footprints you'll see.

Note: All Turks & Caicos Island beaches are public, and even the most developed residential beaches are required to have public access points. These access routes are for public use; never cross private property to get to a beach.

PROVIDENCIALES

Starting at Leeward and running all the way to Thompson Cove, **Grace Bay Beach** ✸✸✸ is Provo's finest beach, stretching for 19km

Horseback Riding on the Beach

The dusty dirt road leads up into the Long Bay Hills, home of **Provo Ponies**, which offers **horseback rides on the beach** 🐎🐎 for novices and seasoned riders alike. The Provo Ponies stables comprise a real menagerie, with friendly dogs roaming, roosters crowing, and 18 horses—technically big ponies—available to ride.

On our afternoon ride, we were assigned horses according to skill levels. I'm a less-experienced rider, so I was given a lumbering but game animal named Lightning—as in "struck by," as opposed to "fast as." Let's just say Lightning's days as a Triple Crown threat are behind him. But even this old gentleman picked up the pace when we hit the beach; the horses love the gentle sand, the cool breezes, the open spaces. As do the riders: It's a relaxing, soul-satisfying experience.

Camille Slattery, the energetic owner of Provo Ponies, came to the Turks & Caicos 19 years ago to teach scuba diving and never left. Her stable grew along with her love of horses; she opened to the public in 2002. Many of her horses are Grand Turk horses, which Camille calls "bomb-proof: so easy and so intelligent." A couple she even refers to as "babysitters"—they literally take care of the people riding them. These horses can take the heat because they're born and bred here; still, the stable doesn't schedule any midday rides, for the benefit of both horse and rider. Provo Ponies offers two rides a day along the secluded, untrammeled Long Bay beach, in morning and late afternoon. Rides last an hour or 80 minutes, and helmets, fanny packs, and water are provided. They take beginners or experts—and only allow cantering if the rider shows he or she is experienced. They also offer private swimming rides. What is it about riding a horse on a tropical beach? As Camille says, "It's everybody's fantasy." For more information, call ℂ **649/941-5252** or go to www. provo.net/provoponies (Long Bay Hills, off Dolphin Lane; 1-hr. ride $75, 80-min. ride $85; hotel pickup/drop-off included; rides Mon–Sat 9:30am and 4:30pm; 11 riders maximum per trip; maximum 200-lb. weight limit and no children under 5).

Exploring Providenciales & the Caicos Islands

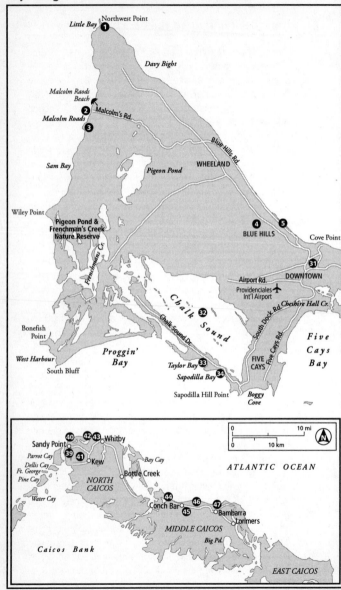

PROVIDENCIALES
Amanyara **3**
Art Provo **14**
Ayurveda Spa **9**
Bamboo Gallery **20**
Bambooz Bar & Grill **27**
Beaches Turks & Caicos
    Resort **10**
Belongings **23**
BET Soundstage **26**
Bight Reef **9**
The Blue Hills **4**
Blue Hills Artisan Studio **5**
The Caicos Conch Farm **18**
Caicos Wear **20**
Chalk Sound **32**
Club Sodax **30**
Danny Buoy's **25**
Dive Provo **23**
Gilley's **16**
Grace Bay Beach **8**
Jean Taylor Gallery **24**
Leeward Marina **17**

Little Water Cay
    (Iguana Island) **15**
Long Bay Beach **21**
The Lounge at the
    Grace Bay Club **13**
Maison Creole **20**
Malcolm Beach **2**
Middle Caicos Co-op **46**
Northwest Point **1**
Phillip Outten **29**
Plunge Bar **11**
Ports of Call **23**
Provo Golf &
    Country Club **19**
Provo Ponies **22**
Pulse Gym **27**
Royal Jewels **31**
The Saltmills **27**
Sapodilla Bay **34**
Serenity Spa **28**
Smith's Reef **6**
The Spa at the Palms **11**
Spa Tropique **23**

Taylor Bay **33**
The Thalasso Spa at
    Point Grace **12**
Turks & Caicos National
    Trust Shop **24**
Turtle Cove Marina **7**
Unicorn Bookstore **28**

NORTH CAICOS
Horsestable Beach **43**
Pelican Point **42**
Sandy Point **39**
Three Mary Cays **40**
Wades Green
    Plantation **41**

MIDDLE CAICOS
Bambarra Beach **47**
Conch Bar Caves
    National Park **45**
The Crossing Place
    Trail **46**
Mudjin Harbor **44**

Caicos Watersports Operators: Master List

Watersports activities are the name of the game in the Turks & Caicos, and in most cases you'll be availing yourself of the capable expertise of local watersports operators and boat charters to get out and play in the miles of sea, whether you're on a scuba-diving or snorkeling expedition, parasailing or sailing, enjoying an eco-adventure, visiting other islands, or simply taking one of the extremely popular beach excursions that combine any number of beach activities. Much of the coral reef is protected national parkland and the waters are too shallow in spots to allow powerboats and personal watercraft to be rented out without a captain aboard—with a few exceptions, in designated spots. **Sun & Fun Seasports** (✆ **649/946-5724**) rents out motorboats and personal watercraft.

Many of the "beach excursion" boat trips are half-day or daylong cruises that offer a variety of activities, from snorkeling and shelling to beach barbecues, conch diving, and visits to Little Water Cay, or "Iguana Island," as it's also known, a nature reserve where a population of endangered native rock iguanas enjoys protected status (see "A Visit to Iguana Island," later in this chapter).

The following is a master list of the top watersports and charter-boat operators in Providenciales and the Caicos Islands, their contact information, and a general description of the types of services they have to offer. Most include free pickup/drop-off from your hotel to the marina and back in the price of the excursions.

- **Art Pickering's Provo Turtle Divers** (✆ **649/946-4232**; www. provoturtledivers.com): Scuba diving, instruction, and equipment rental; snorkeling.
- *Beluga* **Charter Sailing** (✆ **649/946-4396**; www.sailbeluga. com): Captained charter sailing on a Polynesian catamaran; beach excursions.
- **Big Blue Unlimited** (✆ **649/946-5034**; www.bigblue unlimited.com): Technical and recreational scuba diving,

(12 miles) of spectacular, powdery-soft white sand. The gin-clear, crystal-blue waters are extremely tranquil and have no rocks, making it an ideal playground for kids. Resorts and hotels have developed

instruction, and equipment rental; eco-adventures (including kayaking, snorkeling, mountain biking, and North Caicos trips); private charters.

- **Caicos Adventures** (© 649/941-3346; www.tcidiving. com): Scuba diving, instruction, and equipment rental.
- **Catch the Wave** (© 649/941-3047; www.tcimall.tc/ catchthewave/default.htm): Bonefishing and bottom fishing; beach excursions; water-skiing; island safaris (including cave and bird-watching trips); private charters.
- **Dive Provo** (© 800/234-7768 in the U.S. or 649/946-5040; www.diveprovo.com): Technical and recreational scuba diving, instruction, and equipment rental; hotel/dive packages; snorkeling.
- **J&B Tours** (© 649/946-5047; www.jbtours.com): Beach excursions, cruises, and barbecues; bonefishing, bottom fishing, and deep-sea fishing; snorkeling; island getaways; glowworm cruises; cave safaris.
- **Ocean Vibes** (© 649/231-6636; www.oceanvibes.com): Scuba diving, instruction, and equipment rental; scuba and snorkeling charters; multiday packages.
- **Reef Peepers** (© 649/941-8605; www.reefpeepers.com): Glass-bottom-boat excursions; snorkeling trips; sunset wine-and-cheese cruises; private charters.
- **Sail Provo** (© 649/946-4783; www.sailprovo.com): Sailing cruises; snorkeling cruises; combination beach excursion cruises; glowworm cruises; sunset cruises; weddings.
- **Silver Deep** (© 649/946-5612; www.silverdeep.com): Scuba diving; snorkeling; bonefishing, bottom fishing, fly-fishing, deep-sea fishing, night fishing, and shark fishing; beach excursions and barbecues; glowworm cruises; sunset cruises; island getaways; private charters.
- **Sun Charters** (© 649/231-0624; www.suncharters.tc): Sailing cruises and beach excursions aboard the *Atabeyra;* pirate cruises; private charters; weddings.

along its edge, but in many places along the shoreline, you'll have these sands all to yourself. Though there are no public facilities on the beach, the hotels themselves come in handy because all of them have restrooms and bars serving tropical drinks. Smith's Reef, near the Turtle Cove Marina, and Bight Reef, directly in front of the Reef Residences/Coral Gardens, are two excellent snorkeling spots right on Grace Bay.

Grace Bay Beach is so stunning that you might not want to venture anywhere else, but a few other beaches on the island are worth a look. In the east, **Long Bay Beach** lies on the opposite shore from Grace Bay, opening onto Long Bay itself. It begins around Juba Point and extends east to Stubbs Cove and is virtually free of hotels (but is a growing residential area). The shallow waters here are very sheltered and have virtually no waves, making it perfect for young children. Take a horseback ride on the beach here with Provo Ponies (see box in this section).

If you really crave privacy, seek out **Malcolm Beach.** The traditional way to see this charming cove (often referred to as Malcolm Roads Beach) is by 4×4 along twisting, bumpy Malcolm Roads. You can also access the beach by staying at Amanyara (the resort is adjacent to the beach) or by getting a tour-boat operator to take you there. Its waters are part of the Northwest Point Marine National Park. There's good snorkeling, though you'll have to bring your own gear—unless, of course, you're a guest at Amanyara, which has excellent snorkeling and other watersports equipment.

Chalk Sound, a landlocked lagoon west of Five Cays Settlement, has been turned into a public park. The hamlet of Five Cays itself boasts a small harbor and a modern airport. **Sapodilla Bay** and **Taylor Bay** are part of Chalk Sound National Park. These beautiful, shallow bays along Provo's southwest coastline have soft, silty bottoms and warm water. Sapodilla Bay lies between two 9m (30-ft.) cliffs at Gussy Cove, stretching all the way west to Ocean Point. This is such a well-protected beach—with fine sands and clear shallow water (even 30m/98 ft. out)—that the locals often refer to it as "the children's beach."

CAICOS CAYS

Pine Cay's perfect crescent of pale white sand is rimmed by azure seas. This private island is also home to **The Meridian Club** (p. 79) and a number of private homes. **Parrot Cay** is another gorgeous private island, this one with an eponymous resort with a celebrity clientele and fabulous spa.

You may touch down on one of the lovely uninhabited cays of the Caicos Cays with one of the many half- or full-day beach excursions offered by a number of watersports operators in the area. Many of these cays are part of TCI national parkland. Among them are **Little Water Cay,** a nature reserve that is home to a population of native rock iguanas (see "A Visit to Iguana Island," later in this chapter); **Fort George Cay,** a National Historic Site; and **Dellis Cay,** where you can find sand dollars half-buried in the shallows. All have beautiful, fine-powder beaches.

NORTH CAICOS

Up until now, only those in the know found their way to **Sandy Point,** a crescent of perfect beach within sight of the Parrot Cay resort. All that is soon to change: Ground was broken in 2006 for construction of the Royal Reef Resort, a luxury hotel and condos fronting the beach.

Just east of Sandy Point, the coves of **Three Mary Cays** (named for its three distinctive rocks) are prime snorkeling spots. In Whitby, step into the shallows of the palm-fringed **Pelican Point beach** (in front of Pelican Beach Hotel) and find conch shells of every size. Also in Whitby, lovely **Horsestable Beach** has enjoyed its North Caicos seclusion for years (it's also a prime bird-watching spot); now it's the future home of the $70-million St. Charles condominium resort.

MIDDLE CAICOS

The soft green cliffs overlooking the sea in **Mudjin Harbor** provide a dramatic departure from the dry, flat scrublands of Provo. Down below, Dragon Cay has coves set amid turquoise shallows that make for perfect snorkeling and swimming. Travel along the old Conch Bar on bluffs above the shoreline until you reach **Bambarra Beach,** where casuarina pines fringe a white-sand beach; at low tide a long sandbar stretches from the beach to Pelican Cay.

2 Scuba Diving & Snorkeling

SCUBA DIVING 🐠🐠🐠

Dive experts, including the late Jacques Cousteau, have cited Providenciales as one of the 10 best sites in the world. Why is the diving so good in Provo and the Turks & Caicos in general? A number of reasons: great visibility (often more than 30m/100 ft.), gentle seas, a barrier reef that runs the full length of the island's 27km (17-mile) north coast, dramatic vertical underwater "walls" where the coral is big and healthy and marine life congregates, and a local government committed to protecting its natural assets—much of the coastal

> ### ⓘ Tips   Websites for Divers
>
> For useful information on scuba diving in the Caribbean, check out the website of the **Professional Association of Diving Instructors (PADI)** at **www.padi.com**. This site provides descriptions of dive destinations throughout the Caribbean and a directory of PADI-certified dive operators. *Scuba Diving Magazine* also has a helpful website at **www.scubadiving.com**. Both sites list dive-package specials and display gorgeous color photos of some of the most beautiful dive spots in the world.

waters around Provo are protected national parkland, where fishing is not allowed. The water is warm and calm much of the year.

From the shore at Grace Bay, visitors can see where the sea breaks along 23km (14 miles) of barrier reef, the teeming undersea home to sea life that ranges from swarms of colorful schools of fish to barracuda to rotund grouper.

Around Provo and the Caicos Islands, the popular diving spots include **Grace Bay, Northwest Point** (a 4.8km/3-mile strip of excellent dive sites with a vertical drop-off to 2,099m/6,888 ft.); **Pine Cay; West Caicos** (with miles of 1,829m/6,000-ft. vertical walls); and **French Cay** (more 6,000-ft. vertical drop-offs). The latter two are great spots to see large pelagics such as reef sharks, sea turtles, stingrays, and dolphins. For extensive information about each of these sites, go to the very informative website of **Art Pickering's Provo Turtle Divers Ltd.,** Turtle Cove (ⓒ **649/946-4232,** or 800/833-1341 for reservations; www.provoturtledivers.com), the oldest dive operation in the islands.

Most dive operators rent scuba tanks, plus backpacks and weight belts (included in the dive cost). In general, a single-tank dive costs $75, a night dive goes for $75, and a morning two-tank dive is $109. Many offer technical diving and PADI training, with full instruction and resort courses. An open-water PADI referral course goes for $400.

SNORKELING 𝕽𝕽𝕽
The snorkeling is as good as it is on Provo and the Caicos Islands for the same reasons the diving is exalted (see above). This is a great place to learn to snorkel—the waters are clean, clear, temperate, and gentle—and the marine life is rich and thriving.

A number of watersports operators offer snorkeling trips (or combination snorkeling/beach excursions) off Grace Bay or in and around the Caicos Cays, a short (30-min.) trip from Leeward Marina (see "Caicos Watersports Operators: Master List," above). **Caicos Adventures** takes you farther still, on 4.6m-wide (15-ft.) powered catamarans, to superb snorkeling spots in West Caicos and French Cay, both about an hour's boat ride from Leeward (© **649/ 941-3346;** www.caicosadventures.com).

You can even find great snorkeling opportunities right on Grace Bay. While most resorts along Grace Bay offer complimentary snorkeling equipment with which you can happily tool around the clear shallows in front of your hotel, it's unlikely that you'll see anything other than the clear turquoise sea and a sprinkling of pink-tinged sunrise tellins or sun-bleached coral. If you really want to see an active underwater marine garden, grab your snorkeling equipment and head down the beach to one of Grace Bay's two prime snorkeling spots, **Smith's Reef** and **Bight Reef,** both in the Princess Alexandra National Park, off the northwest corner of Provo.

Smith's Reef, near Turtle Cove Marina, a walk-in dive to a seascape of brain and fan corals, purple gorgonians, anemones, sea cucumbers, sergeant majors, green parrotfish, long-nosed trumpet fish, the ominous-looking green moray, an occasional southern ray, and a visiting hawksbill turtle or two. Smith's Reef has underwater signs that describe the coral reef ecosystem and the diversity of life that thrives there. Snorkelers can learn about the various creatures camouflaged within the reef, the importance of sea-grass beds, and the ways that parrotfish contribute to the environment. The trail follows the perimeter of the reef starting inshore in about 1m to 2m (3¼–6½ ft.) of water, increasing to 7m to 9m (23–30 ft.) deep. The depth marks a spectacular display of coral creations, colorful schooling fish, and spotted eagle rays; even resident turtles can be found.

Even closer than Smith's Reef to most guests staying on Grace Bay, Bight Reef is located in the Grace Bay area known as the Bight, just offshore the Reef Residences/Coral Gardens. A public footpath leads to the beach, and two marker buoys indicate both ends of the snorkel trail. The **Bight Reef Snorkel Trail** has underwater trail signs that describe corals and how they grow. Water depth ranges from 1m to 5m (3¼–16 ft.), and visitors can view mobile species like yellowtail snappers, big jolthead porgies, and sand-sifting mojarras. You can get snorkeling equipment (and even diving lessons) at **Cactus Voyager,** the in-house dive operator in the Reef Residences on Grace Bay, directly in front of the reef (© **649/941-3713**).

On **North Caicos** the snorkeling is especially good at Three Mary Cays, a marine sanctuary just east of Sandy Point and part of 11km-long (7-mile) Whitby Beach. On **Middle Caicos** you can snorkel in Mudjin Harbor around Dragon Cay.

3 Beach Excursions & Boat Charters

One of the most popular watersports activities in the Provo area is a **beach excursion** 𝕬𝕬𝕬 offered by a number of charter-boat operators. These excursions come in any number of variations and combinations, and in many instances you can personally tailor your own excursion or hire a private charter to take you to a secluded cay for the day.

Charter boats leave out of Leeward Marina (on Provo's northeast shore)—and most operators include hotel or resort pickup and drop-off in the price of your excursion.

A favorite beach excursion is a half-day or full day out on the Caicos Cays that includes **snorkeling,** a visit to **Iguana Island** (see below), and a **shelling stopover** on one of the uninhabited cays. Other variations include **conch diving** (you can try to dive the 6m/20-ft. depths, but most people let the expert guides do the diving

A Visit to Iguana Island

Many of the beach excursions to the Caicos Cays include a short tour of **Little Water Cay** 𝕬𝕬, a protected nature reserve (part of the Princess Alexandra National Park) and home to the **Turks & Caicos rock iguana,** a small, harmless reptile that is found nowhere else on the planet. Boardwalks and observation towers have been constructed at two popular landing sites to reduce the impact of tourism—this is, after all, one of the most popular attractions in the Turks & Caicos. As you walk along the wooden boardwalks that crisscross the 47-hectare (116-acre) island, you'll spot members of the island iguana population, here some 3,000 strong, emerging from their sand burrows. The biggest of these iguanas are more than .6m (2 ft.) long and solid; they're handsome fellows, if you like the rough-and-ready type, and literally rule the roost. The rock iguanas of Turks & Caicos are the islands' largest native land animal—even so, they're no match for a number of predators, including cats. About 50,000 rock iguanas remain here, the largest and healthiest population in the Caribbean. A park access fee of $5 per visitor is charged to help support further conservation activities.

to retrieve fresh conch) and a subsequent lunch of fresh conch salad, prepared on the spot seviche-style; **beach barbecues** or **picnics;** or **sunset cruises** with wine and cheese.

On a **glowworm cruise,** boats take you out around sunset 4 or 5 days after a full moon to see millions of mating glowworms light up the shallow local waters with a glittering green glow.

More ambitious beach excursions include **"island safaris"** and **ecotours** in North or Middle Caicos, trips that may combine boating and snorkeling with caving, bird-watching, kayaking, biking, hiking, visiting historic sites, or having lunch in a native home. **Big Blue Unlimited** (© 649/946-5034; www.bigblueunlimited.com) is highly recommended for its creative ecotours.

A number of watersports operators offer **private charters,** whether for personalized island touring or just a pickup or drop-off on another island.

For contact information on recommended operators who offer excellent beach excursions and private charters, go to the "Caicos Watersports Operators: Master List," earlier in this chapter.

4 Sailing, Parasailing & Other Watersports

SAILING   Sailing excursions are offered by many charter groups, most notably **Sail Provo** (© 649/946-4783; www.sailprovo.com/contact.htm). It sails 14m or 15m (48- or 52-ft.) catamarans on

---

Spotting JoJo the Dolphin

JoJo, a wild Atlantic bottlenose dolphin, is a local celebrity here and acts like one, showing off for visitors as he plays in the waters of Grace Bay. He's even a movie star, having appeared in *Nature* and *In the Wild: Dolphins,* both PBS specials, and the 2000 IMAX film *Dolphins.* He's so famous he's been named a Turks & Caicos National Treasure and as such enjoys protected status. He likes to trail boats, and sightings of JoJo in the clear Grace Bay sea happen almost daily. A whole cottage industry of all things JoJo has sprung up. You can learn more about JoJo and the JoJo Project on the website of the **Marine Wildlife Foundation** (www.marinewildlife.org), which is dedicated to the research and preservation of dolphins, whales, and all marine wildlife. A bell at Hemingway's on the Beach oceanfront restaurant at The Sands at Grace Bay resort is there for anyone to ring if they spot JoJo.

> **Kids Day Pass at Beaches**
>
> Even if you're not staying there, you can treat yourself and your family to a day's worth of all the resort activities, meals and drinks, and encounters with *Sesame Street* characters you can possibly stand with a day pass to the all-inclusive **Beaches Turks & Caicos Resort & Spa.** The cost is $120 per adult ($60 per child) and lasts from 9am until 5pm. It's an especially fun option for the small kids in your party who are gaga for all things Elmo and Cookie Monster—and not a bad day at the beach for older kids who have total access to Beaches' wealth of sports and watersports facilities and Xbox Game Oasis Center. Turn to chapter 3 for a rundown of all the activities that Beaches has to offer. For more information, call ⓒ **649/946-8000.**

half- or full-day excursions. One of the most frequented is a sailing and snorkeling trip for $63 that's offered on Monday, Wednesday, and Saturday and includes a tour of Little Water Cay, or "Iguana Island." A full-day cruise Tuesday to Friday costs $125, including a lunch buffet served onboard. Sail Provo also offers sunset cruises and glowworm cruises.

A retired rumrunner, *Atabeyra,* is owned by **Sun Charters** (ⓒ **649/231-0624;** www.suncharters.tc). Full-day trips cost $75 and include an afternoon buffet and take you down the chain of Caicos Cays, perhaps following an ocean trail blazed by Columbus.

Sail aboard the catamaran *Beluga* (ⓒ **649/946-4396;** www.sailbeluga.com) with Captain Tim Ainley on small, personally tailored beach excursions or private charters for romantic beach barbecues.

PARASAILING   You won't see jet skis blazing across Grace Bay, but you will see the occasional billowy parasail high up in the air, casting shadows on the aquamarine seas. Your best bet is to call on **Captain Marvin's Parasailing,** Grace Bay (ⓒ **649/231-0643;** www.captainmarvinsparasail.com). A 15-minute flight over beautiful Grace Bay costs $70. You can also take a banana-boat ride at $25 per person or go water-skiing for $70 per person.

OTHER WATERSPORTS   Windsurfing & Kite-Boarding You can get kite-boarding and windsurfing lessons and/or equipment rentals at **Windsurfing Provo on the Beach** (Ocean Club East & Ocean Club West, Grace Bay, Providenciales; ⓒ **649/941-1687;** www.windsurfingprovo.tc). You can also rent kayaks and boogie boards here.

5 Fishing

The fishing is excellent in the Turks & Caicos, whether bonefishing, reef fishing, deep-sea fishing, or bottom fishing. A number of reputable boat-charter companies offer fishing expeditions; go to the "Caicos Watersports Operators: Master List," earlier in this chapter, for contact information. **Silver Deep** (© 649/941-5441; www. silverdeep.com) offers fishing excursions, with both half- and full-day expeditions, usually for bonefishing or bottom fishing. Tackle and bait are included.

For those who'd like to venture farther afield—and pay a lot more money—half- and full-day deep-sea fishing expeditions are available, with all equipment included. Catches turn up wahoo, tuna, kingfish, marlin, and even shark.

In Middle Caicos, **Cardinal Arthur** (© 649/946-6107; cell-phone 649/241-0730) is a one-man fishing charter. The sixth-generation Middle Caicos native can take you fishing for snapper, grouper, grunt, or barracuda.

6 Golf & Tennis

GOLF   Provo Golf & Country Club ⊛, on Grace Bay Road (© 649/946-5833; www.provogolfclub.com), is one of only two golf courses in the country (the other is on Grand Turk). The 6,560-yard, par-72, 18-hole course was designed by Karl Litten of Boca Raton, Florida, and is owned by the Turks and Caicos Water Company. It is powerfully green and—because Provo is one of the driest spots on the globe—it takes an extraordinary amount of water to keep it that way. Young palms and bougainvillea, as well as rocky outcroppings and powdery sand traps, help make the course a challenge to the serious golfer or a lovely day on the links for the beginner or novice. Four sets of tees allow golfers to tailor a game to their level of expertise. A driving range and putting greens are also available. Inside the clubhouse is a full-service restaurant and bar called **Fairways Bar & Grill** (p. 93). Greens fees are $140 per person for 18 holes. The price includes the use of a shared golf cart, which is mandatory. Golf clubs can be rented for $20 to $40 per set. The course is open from 7am to 7:30pm daily. The course also has two lighted hard tennis courts (see below). Inside the clubhouse is the Pro Shop, a fully stocked store with golf and tennis equipment as well as tennis and golf shoes, collared shirts, tailored shorts, and hats.

Nakier Wilson's Favorite TCI Experiences

Nakier Wilson is a Belonger (a native-born Turks islander) who knows just about anyone and everyone on the islands—which makes her job, as public-relations officer for the Turks & Caicos Tourist Board, a perfect fit. Nakier puts great stock in going to places where the vibe is laid-back and relaxed. Here are Nakier's favorite TCI experiences:

- "My favorite restaurant is **Da Conch Shack.** The name is self-explanatory: You get conch prepared any way you want it (fried, grilled, fresh out of the water, and so many other ways). The atmosphere is relaxing, with little shaded huts directly on beautiful Blue Hills Beach."
- "My favorite thing to do on a weekend or holiday is go **sailing with the crew from Sail Provo.** I like the evening-sunset-cruise package from 4 to 7pm. It gets to be quite adventurous when we sail around the northeast side of Providenciales."
- "At night I like to unwind at the **Bambooz Bar & Grill** or . . .
- ". . . at the **BET Soundstage,** which has a live DJ who plays a wide range of music."
- "Occasionally I'll set an appointment to visit the **Spa** at Reef Residences/Coral Gardens), where I always get the Exotic Coconut Rub and Milk Wrap—which can be only described as pure pleasure."

TENNIS   Many of Provo's hotels and resorts have on-site tennis courts, including Beaches, Club Med, the Grace Bay Club, the Ocean Club, The Palms, and The Sands at Grace Bay. The **Provo Golf & Country Club** has two lighted hard courts that the public is welcome to reserve ($10 per person per hour; reserve 24 hr. in advance; open daily 7am–7:30pm).

7 Attractions & Tours

PROVIDENCIALES

Provo has little in the way of historic or cultural attractions; for a real feel for the rich heritage of the TCI, you'll need to head to

North or Middle Caicos (see below) and, of course, to Grand Turk and Salt Cay (see chapter 6).

The Caicos Conch Farm 𝔖   The Conch Farm is located on the isolated eastern end of the island, amid a flat and sunbaked terrain of scrub and sand. This is the only place in the world where conch is commercially produced. Although it was first built as a research facility, the farm not only exports much of the conch you eat in the Florida Keys and Miami, but its breeding techniques could help save the conch from extinction—it's a real venture in eco-mariculture. Its stated mission is to "help provide jobs, stimulate economic growth, supply a low-cost source of protein, and protect wild conch stocks from exploitation." Conch has many natural predators—man is at the top of the list—and only a tiny percentage of hatched conch eggs survive in the wild, whereas 25% of the eggs survive here in this controlled environment. The Turks islanders staff gives visitors a short walking tour of the breeding basins—included is a tour of the hatchery and the laboratories, where more than two million conch reside in ponds in various stages of growth. The tour is modest, but the passion for the cause is palpable. This is truly a hands-on enterprise: It is someone's job to hand-feed food pellets to most of the young conch daily. A gift shop sells rare conch pearls, shell jewelry, and T-shirts.

Heaving Down Rock, Leeward Hwy., Providenciales. ⓒ **649/946-5330.** www. caicosconchfarm.com. Admission $6 adults, $3 children. Mon–Fri 9am–4pm; Sat 9am–2pm.

NORTH CAICOS

A number of charter-boat operators offer island tours, ecotours, bird-watching tours, or private charters to North Caicos, including **J&B Tours** (ⓒ **649/946-5047;** www.jbtours.com) and **Big Blue Unlimited** (ⓒ **649/946-5034;** www.bigblueunlimited.com). Big Blue combines boat rides with bike trips, kayaking, bird-watching, and lunches in native homes to get deep into the North Caicos experience. You many even get to **Flamingo Pond,** tidal flats on the island's south side and home to the largest protected nature sanctuary of West Indian flamingos in the islands.

Wades Green Plantation   North Caicos became plantation country when Americans loyal to the British crown (Loyalists) fled the United States to come here, where they were provided property from the British crown, in the wake of the War of Independence. According to historians at the Turks & Caicos National Museum, in

1788 the Caicos Islands had a population of over 40 white families and 1,200 slaves. All slaves were freed in 1834, and today many descendants of these slaves reside in North Caicos. The main industry on these plantations was growing sea-island cotton, an endeavor that eventually failed as a result of dry conditions, thin soil, pests, and tropical storms. Today you can still see the occasional cotton plant growing tall along the roadside in both North and Middle Caicos. Outside of Kew are the ruins of one of the most successful plantations of the Loyalist era, Wades Green, which was constructed by Florida Loyalist Wade Stubbs around 1789 and eventually grew to 1,214 hectares (3,000 acres). Today you can see the ruins of the stone house, outbuildings, and surrounding walls, pillowed in North Caicos scrub brush. Call the Turks & Caicos National Trust for tours.

Kew, North Caicos. © 649/946-5710. tc.natrust@tciway.tc.

MIDDLE CAICOS

Catch the Wave (© 649/941-3047; www.tcimall.tc/catchthewave/default.htm) offers island safaris to Middle Caicos, including cave and bird-watching safaris. **J&B Tours** (© 649/946-5047; www.jbtours.com) offers cave safaris and beach picnics on Middle Caicos. Middle Caicos native and guide **Cardinal Arthur** (© 649/946-6107; cellphone 649/241-0730) offers cave, bird-watching, fishing, and ecotours and general sightseeing trips of the island. Also offering cave tours (and good general sightseeing tours) is local guide **Ernest Forbes, Sr.** (© 649/946-6140).

Conch Bar Caves National Park 🐾   These cool limestone caves are a surprising treat to discover on the flat, sunbaked TCI. This massive (24km/15-mile) aboveground limestone cave system (with 3.2km/2 miles of surveyed caves) was used by pre-Columbian Lucayan Indians more than 600 years ago—a number of artifacts from their occupation are housed in the Turks & Caicos National Museum. Today it's basically a big bat cave (mined for exported guano back in the late 19th c.), with impressive stalactites, stalagmites, flowstone, and pools. Look for land crabs around the entrance to the caves. *Tip:* Spray yourself thoroughly with mosquito repellent before you go in. For more information, contact the **Turks & Caicos National Trust** (© 649/946-5710).

The Crossing Place Trail 🐾   This lovely coastal route, much of it along a bluff overlooking the azure waters of Mudjin Harbor, was first established in the late 1700s by cotton plantation settlers. As part of the Turks & Caicos National Trust Middle Caicos Ecotourism

Project, it has been reopened from the Conch Bar to the Indian Cave field road. (Crossing Place refers to the place where in years past people crossed the sand bars at low tide to get to North Caicos.) During the days of the Loyalist plantations, the owners rode along the King's Road while the slaves walked the trail. You can hike or bike this trail; go to **www.tcimall.tc/middlecaicos/crossingplace. htm** for more information on hiking and biking routes. The trail is generally flat, with some low hills. For more information, contact the **Turks & Caicos National Trust** (© **649/946-5710**).

8 Spas & Gyms

The resorts of Providenciales and the Caicos Cays have some of the finest spas in the Caribbean region—and for many, you don't even have to be a guest to take advantage of some truly splendid treatments. (You'll need to reserve any spa treatment in advance, of course.) *Note:* Unfortunately, **COMO Shambhala** at Parrot Cay is not able to accommodate nonguests at this time.

If you don't want to go the resort route, I recommend the spa treatments offered at **Serenity Spa,** now located in suites 201 and 202 in the Graceway House (adjacent to the IGA) on Leeward Highway (© **649/946-5010;** www.serenity-spa.com; Mon–Sat 9am–6pm); or **Spa Tropique** (© **649/231-6938;** www.spatropique. com; hours vary), which has a location in the Ports of Call shopping plaza and even makes house calls—try its Body Tropique product line, made with local ingredients like sea salt.

Here is a sampling of some of the top resort spas in the TCI that welcome nonguests. Be sure to ask whether a service charge has been added to the bill automatically (some places automatically tack on service charges up to 18%).

AYURVEDA SPA   This day spa is undergoing an expansion as part of the $6-million renovation that is adding the Reef Residences/Coral Gardens resort. The emphasis is on the ancient Indian system of ayurvedic medicine, a holistic approach to mind/body wellness that uses herbs, vegetables, and minerals as healing properties. Choose from basic massages to body scrubs to ayurvedic-specific treatments. The spa is open daily from 9am to 9pm (Reef Residences on Grace Bay, Providenciales; © **649/941-3713**, ext. 3201), and massages start at $60.

THE SPA AT THE PALMS   You'll feel better just stepping into this place, which is elegant and soothing all at once. It's simply a beautiful space, classically designed around reflecting pools. Some of the treatment rooms are set in alfresco coral-stone cabanas shaded by palm trees. The menu of services is extensive and includes facials, massages, body scrubs and other therapies, and day retreat packages (The Palms resort, Grace Bay, Providenciales; © **649/946-8666,** ext. 30308 or 30211; www.thepalmstc.com). Massages start at $80; open daily from 8am to 8pm.

THE THALASSO SPA AT POINT GRACE This full-service oceanfront European-style thalassotherapy spa uses the properties of seawater as well as applications of sea mud and select seaweed in its body and facial treatments. The ambience is dreamy: outdoors in an open-air structure with views of the beach. The menu includes Swedish massage, shiatsu, body scrubs, and wraps (Point Grace Resort, Providenciales; © **649/946-5096,** ext. 4126). Open daily from 9am to 6pm. Massages start at $75.

GYMS

Many resorts have on-site gyms or fitness centers. For those that don't, **Pulse Gym** (The Saltmills, Grace Bay Rd.; © 649/941-8686) is open 7 days a week and has Cybex strength and cardio equipment, free weights, and exercise, Pilates, and yoga classes.

9 Shopping

Providenciales and the Caicos Islands are still a work in progress when it comes to shopping, with no malls to speak of, just a few small shopping "villages" or plazas generally either on Grace Bay Road or Leeward Highway. The most prominent of these are the **Saltmills** (Grace Bay Rd.), which has seven shops, including a wine-and-liquor store, and several restaurants; and **Ports of Call** (Grace Bay Rd.), with eight shops and several restaurants.

You may not be shopping until you drop during your TCI vacation, but you can discover some real gems if you do some digging—particularly when it comes to regional artwork, much of it reasonably priced and including the famously colorful paintings by artists from neighboring Haiti, as well as local crafts, such as beautifully made Middle Caicos fanner-grass baskets and silvertop-palm bags, hats, and other items.

Most shops are open from 9 or 10am to 5 or 6pm (generally later in the high season). Be sure to call in advance so you aren't disappointed to find that a store has shut down for the day.

ARTWORK

Art Provo ☆   This art gallery has a large selection of paintings by local artists, Turks & Caicos pottery, baskets, jewelry, and glass. Look for local painters like Dwight Outten (cousin to Phillip; see below), a Middle Caicos native whose clean-lined, realistic oil paintings of the region are particularly fine. A popular Salt Cay artist represented here, Trevor Morgan, died of sickle cell anemia in 2006 at the age of 29. Ocean Club Plaza, Grace Bay Rd., Providenciales. ☏ **649/941-4545.** www.art provo.com.

Bamboo Gallery ☆   One of the island's leading art galleries moved in 2006 from its longtime location in the Market Place shopping plaza on Leeward Highway to a more high-traffic tourist area on Grace Bay Road. Most of its inventory is comprised of colorful oil paintings by Haitian artists like the popular Ben Oduma. Some local artists are represented, including Phillip Outten. Caicos Café Plaza, Grace Bay Rd., Providenciales. ☏ **649/946-4748.**

Jean Taylor Gallery   This artist sells his colorful, people-filled paintings in this modest gallery in the middle of Grace Bay. You can find him here working on his paintings when he's not cooking at Danny Buoy's, next door. Grace Bay Plaza, Grace Bay Rd., Providenciales. ☏ **649/231-2708.**

Maison Creole   This shop has some lovely Haitian arts and crafts, including hand-painted place mats and boxes. Maison Creole also has a small shop in the international-departures lounge at the Provo airport. Caicos Café Plaza, Grace Bay Rd., Providenciales. ☏ **649/946-4285.**

Phillip Outten ☆   Off Leeward Highway, look for the sign at the Venetian Road turnoff that says LOCAL ARTISTS STUDIO. Follow the road and more signs to the home of this painter, who also has horses and dogs on the sunbaked property. Just off Venetian Rd., Providenciales. ☏ **649/941-3610** or cellphone 649/241-8246. phillipoutten@tciway.tc.

BOOKS

Unicorn Bookstore   This, the island's only full-service bookstore, has books (bestsellers, fiction, nonfiction, kids' books, and more), newspapers, magazine, and gifts. Leeward Hwy., in front of the IGA Graceway, Providenciales. ☏ **649/941-5458.**

CLOTHING

Caicos Wear   This small clothing store offers a good selection of comfortable casual wear, sundresses, colorful peasant skirts, bathing suits, and bags. La Petite Place, Grace Bay Rd., Grace Bay. ☏ **649/941-3346.**

Dive Provo   This dive operator's shop offers dive trips and snorkeling equipment, plus some surprisingly nice casual tops and shorts that work well in a tropical clime. Ports of Call shopping plaza, Grace Bay Rd., Providenciales. © 649/946-5040. www.diveprovo.com.

GIFTS/HOME FURNISHINGS

Belongings ✿   This wonderful home-furnishings store meshes a sleek urban design sensibility with breezy island inspirations. You'll find lots you'll want to take home here: from beautiful lamps with mother-of-pearl mosaic bases and reproduced antique book plates to simple, elegant table linens, vases, candle holders, and reversible quilts. Ports of Call shopping plaza. © 649/941-8055. http://belongingstc.com.

HANDICRAFTS

Blue Hills Artisan Studio ✿   This is an outpost of the Middle Caicos Co-op set in a picturesque Blue Hills cottage with a white picket fence. More than 60 Caicos Islands artisans are represented here, where you can purchase fanner-grass baskets of all shapes and sizes and silvertop-palm crafts, including beribboned straw hats. Blue Hills Beach Rd., Providenciales. © 649/941-7639 or 649/232-7639. middle caicos@tciway.tc.

Middle Caicos Co-op ✿✿   Handsome hand-carved model Caicos Islands sailing sloops can be custom-ordered from the Middle Caicos Co-op—sail plan, size, and color schemes all to your specifications. These sloops are carved from the native gum elemi tree, a Caribbean softwood. The co-op also sells fanner-grass baskets, silvertop-palm straw hats, bags, and more, plus Middle Caicos grits. Conch Bar, Middle Caicos. ©/fax 649/946-6132. www.tcimall.tc/middle caicos/co-op.htm or e-mail middlecaicos@tciway.tc.

Turks & Caicos National Trust Shop ✿   Here you can find the real deal: crafts and products made in the Turks & Caicos, including native pottery, fanner-grass baskets, silvertop-palm bags, model Caicos sloops, and more. Get your rock iguana T-shirts here! Grace Bay Plaza, Grace Bay Rd., Providenciales © 649/941-3536. www.nationaltrust.tc.

JEWELRY

Royal Jewels   This duty-free shop has good stocks in gold jewelry and designer watches and French and international perfumes—all that standard showcase stuff found on other islands in the Caribbean. It also has a location in the international-departures lounge in the Provo airport. Arch Plaza, Leeward Hwy., Providenciales. © 649/946-4699.

Shopping the Hotel Boutiques

Shopping doesn't have to stop at your hotel door. A number of hotels and resorts in Provo have very good in-house boutique shops, many selling items you won't find in most standard-issue hotel gift shops. Here are a few recommended shops and a sampling of the goods you might discover there:

- **Amanyara:** This hotel resort on Provo's Northwest Point offers such high-end goodies as Asian-inspired tunic tops by Elizabeth Hurley Beach; Havaianas flip-flops from Brazil; and Amanresorts' wonderful skin-care line and spa products.

- **Beaches:** Beaches has two stores: **Treasure Island,** which sells high-end beachwear, Beaches-branded T-shirts, hats, and beach paraphernalia, gifts, snacks, soft drinks, and limited toiletries; and **Pirate Cove,** which sells *Sesame Street*–branded clothes and toys and other kids' items.

- **The Meridian Club:** This small shop sells Meridian Club T-shirts, tops, and hats, locally crafted basketry, and other gift items.

- **The Palms:** Palm Place, which faces the terrace of restaurant Parallel23, is a real shopping mecca, featuring not one but five boutique shops. **Wish** boutique has upscale clothing, including those sweet little soft cotton tops and skirts from designer James Perse. Next door the **Palm Shop** carries casual logo wear and gift items. **Splash** has beachwear. **Spice** has gourmet snacks and beverages, such as Harry and David chocolate-covered cherries and Miss Vickie's Potato Chips. **Harmony Gallery** sells lots of the home furnishings and pricey little tchotchkes (handblown-glass conch shells, sea-urchin candlesticks, shell-encrusted mirrors) you see around the hotel. (Oh, and you can also buy skin-care products and treatments along with big-ticket yoga- and sleepwear in the **Spa at the Palms.**)

- **Parrot Cay:** The shop sells lovely but pricey jewel-encrusted Asian-style tunics and kurtas, along with other high-end clothing, books, jewelry, bags, and a few essential toiletries. The COMO Shambhala spa's wildly popular Invigorate line of soaps, shampoos, and the like is also on sale here.

10 Nightlife

The nightlife on Provo can't compete with the late-night revelry of, say, Aruba or even Barbados. This is a laid-back kind of place with laid-back pleasures, but it does offer a number of quality nighttime diversions.

Note: The **American Casino** has been demolished to make room for the **Seven Stars** resort on Grace Bay.

BEACH SHACKS

The **beach shacks along Blue Hills Beach** are fun places to drink Turk's Head beer or a little rum, eat conch, and listen to good music.

LOUNGES/BARS/SPORTS BARS

BEACHSIDE BARS   Great Providenciales beachside lounges or bars from which you can watch the sunset include the **Lounge** (Grace Bay Club; ℭ 649/946-5050); the bar/lounge at **Amanyara** (ℭ 649/941-8133); the **Plunge** pool bar (The Palms resort; ℭ 649/946-8666); and any of the **Blue Hills beach shacks** (see the "Dining Da Blue Hills" sidebar, in chapter 4).

GOLF COURSE BAR   The **Fairways Bar** at the Provo Golf & Country Club (ℭ 649/946-5833) is a pleasant place to have a drink and munch on hearty bar food.

IRISH PUB   Provo has its own Irish pub, **Danny Buoy's** (Grace Bay Rd., Providenciales; ℭ 649/946-5921), with a full bar stocked with imported beers on tap, darts, and pool tables. Danny Buoy's also has good food, with dishes from across the pond (bangers and mash, Irish stew) and island fare (jerk chicken).

MARINA BARS   Turtle Cove Marina   This marina in the northwest section of Provo has a good number of jolly, atmospheric dockside bars, many with happy hours (5–7pm); all serve food, both bar snacks and full-service menus. Join in the revelry at **Aqua Bar & Terrace** (ℭ 649/946-4763); **Baci** (ℭ 649/941-3044); **Banana Boat** (ℭ 649/941-5706); the **Tiki Hut Cabana Bar** (ℭ 649/941-5341); and the **Sharkbite Bar & Grill** (ℭ 649/941-5090). Up above Turtle Cove, at the Miramar Resort, is the **Magnolia Wine Bar** (ℭ 649/941-5108), a lounge next to the Magnolia restaurant with bird's-eye views of Provo and the Grace Bay shoreline.

Leeward Marina   Gilley's (ℭ 649/946-5094) has a full bar with both indoor and terrace seating as well as a full-service restaurant serving good island cuisine (including Gilley's Famous Local Grouper Sandwich). Gilley's also has a branch at the Provo airport.

SPORTS BARS   **Club Sodax** is a nice local sports bar with a good mix of locals and tourists (Leeward Hwy., Providenciales; ✆ 649/941-4540). **Bambooz Bar & Grill** (at the Saltmills shopping plaza, Grace Bay Rd.; Providenciales ✆ 649/941-8146) is another popular spot where you can watch sports on big-screen plasma TVs, listen to music, or dine on island fare (peas and rice, blackened grouper, cracked conch) or international cuisine (New York strip, fish and chips, penne alla vodka).

NIGHTCLUBS

The **BET** (Black Entertainment Television) **Soundstage** (Leeward Hwy., Grace Bay, Providenciales; ✆ 649/946-4318) was the first BET Soundstage outside the U.S. (you can also find one in Disney World) and is a popular spot to dance the night away and drink cocktails beneath palm trees. It also has slot machines.

6

The Turks Islands: Grand Turk & Salt Cay

If you think Providenciales is laid-back, you'd better prepare yourself for the *really* relaxed worlds of Grand Turk and Salt Cay. Grand Turk and Salt Cay are low-key charmers that hold vivid architectural remnants of the islands' colonial past. If you love to scuba-dive or snorkel, have a thing for sun-drenched beaches and ridiculously beautiful seas, and crave a relaxed, back-to-basics departure from the chichi boutique-resort scene, a visit to both islands during your vacation is highly recommended.

1 Grand Turk ★★

Grand Turk is the capital of the Turks & Caicos Islands, although it is no longer the financial and business hub of the island nation, having lost that position to Provo. It is no longer the transportation hub either, as Provo receives 95% of the international airplane landings. The island is rather barren and wind-swept, and even though lovely green bluffs top its northwest and eastern shores, don't come here looking for lush tropical foliage. Do consider Grand Turk, however, if you want a destination that's excellent for snorkeling and diving, with luscious white-sand beaches and a friendly, small-town vibe. You might say it's Mayberry by the Sea.

Cockburn Town (*Coe*-burn) is the financial and business center of this tiny (11km×3.2km/7×2 miles) island, where horses and donkeys still roam the streets. You'll find **Governor's Beach** near—you guessed it—the governor's residence, **Waterloo,** on the west coast of the island. It's the best place for swimming. Take time to tour Cockburn Town's **historic section,** particularly Duke and Front streets, where 200-year-old structures built of wood and limestone stand along the waterfront. Stroll the area and soak in the rhythms of Cockburn Town, the vintage architecture behind picket fences

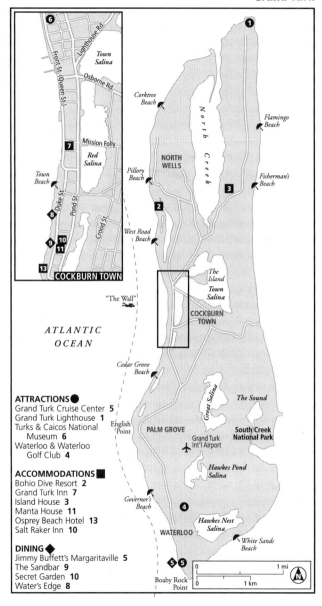

Grand Turk

ATTRACTIONS ●
Grand Turk Cruise Center **5**
Grand Turk Lighthouse **1**
Turks & Caicos National
Museum **6**
Waterloo & Waterloo
Golf Club **4**

ACCOMMODATIONS ■
Bohio Dive Resort **2**
Grand Turk Inn **7**
Island House **3**
Manta House **11**
Osprey Beach Hotel **13**
Salt Raker Inn **10**

DINING ◆
Jimmy Buffett's Margaritaville **5**
The Sandbar **9**
Secret Garden **10**
Water's Edge **8**

The Day the Cruise Ships Came to Town

Grand Turk is the kind of place that lingers with you long after you've left. Maybe that's why some people are concerned that the new kids in town—the Carnival Cruise Line ships that started arriving at the new **Grand Turk Cruise Center** in February 2006—will rend the very fabric that makes this place uniquely quaint. In a 40-year land-lease deal with the TCI government, the cruise line has built a $42-million "tourism village" designed to look like a Bermudian salt-rakers' settlement from the early 19th century. It's a colorful, respectful representation of the local architecture, but its fantastical theme-park underpinnings can't help but peek through. Jimmy Buffett's Margaritaville, for example, is here, bigger, bolder, and brassier than any other Margaritaville on earth, straddled by a lagoon pool with swim-up bars and slides. And silliness reigns when cruise passengers driving multicolored dune buggies parade through the streets of Grand Turk.

Carnival did many wonderful things for Grand Turk in preparation for its opening. Like a good guest, it came in and sort of neatened up the place. It paved the potholed Duke Street area and sandblasted the dirt off the old lighthouse. It brought construction jobs and spiffier taxis to the islands, and locally owned shops opened up in the cruise

entwined with crimson bougainvillea, the fragrant neem trees, the funky beachfront bars, the wet suits hanging out to dry. Stay for a couple of days, and you'll be waving to familiar faces on the street, calling the local dogs by name, and settling into your new favorite spot to watch the sun set over beers on Duke Street.

ESSENTIALS
VISITOR INFORMATION

The **Turks & Caicos Tourist Board** (www.turksandcaicostourism.com) has an office in Grand Turk (Front St., Cockburn Town; ✆ 649/946-2321) and one in New York City (Room 2817, the Lincoln Building, 60 E. 42nd St.; ✆ 800/241-0824). Office hours are Monday to Friday from 8:30am to 4:30pm.

center. It's bringing business to local tour operators, and a nice touch is the horse-drawn carriages that clip-clop through town. On the downside, it cut a hole (albeit an environmentally sensitive one) in the coral reef to build a passage to allow 2,000- to 3,000-passenger ships to dock here. It had "historic" plaques created—the ones now gracing Duke Street's historic inns, restaurants, and the like—but made the mistake of not letting the owners of said places approve the finished products before they hung them up. Many locals were miffed, claiming the plaques were inaccurate, ungrammatical even, and gave much too much personal information about the current owners and not enough actual history. As a result, some owners simply removed the plaques.

Even worse is the fear among the diving community that the cruise ships will foment an environment that is too slick and pricey for the folks who have been coming here for years. Only time will tell, but at press time business appears to be booming in all sectors, and the lovely laid-back rhythms of Grand Turk continue apace.

For more on the cruise center, see "Exploring the Island," below.

GETTING TO GRAND TURK

Your most likely point of entry into the Turks & Caicos Islands will be the **Providenciales International Airport** (www.provoairport. com; p. 40). To get to Grand Turk or Salt Cay, you will be taking a **domestic flight** on one of the interisland airlines (see below) or a charter plane from the Provo airport into Grand Turk International Airport (also known as J.A.G.S. McCartney International Airport). Several daily flights between Provo and Grand Turk are offered by the domestic airlines **SkyKing** (✆ 649/941-3136; www.skyking.tc) and **Air Turks & Caicos** (✆ 649/941-5481 or 649/946-1667 on Grand Turk; www.airturksandcaicos.com). **Global Airways** charters (✆ 649/941-3222; www.globalairways.tc) also flies to Grand Turk.

The flight from Provo to Grand Turk takes 20 minutes and costs approximately $135 round-trip.

As of 2006, **Spirit Airlines** was offering **direct flights** (Sun only) from Fort Lauderdale, Florida, to Grand Turk (© **800/772-7117;** www.spiritair.com/welcome.aspx).

GETTING AROUND GRAND TURK

On Grand Turk you can rent cars (as well as scooters, bicycles, and snorkeling gear) at **Tony's Car Rental** (Grand Turk International Airport; © **649/964-1979;** www.tonyscarrental.com). Cars and jeeps rent for from $70 to $95 a day, scooter rentals cost $40 a day, and bike rentals are $20 a day. Tony's also offers scooter tours of the island.

Taxis are available, but there is no central agency to call. Your hotel can summon one for you, but taxis are always available at the Grand Turk airport. The fare is $10 to $12 from the airport to most major hotels. Drivers are more than happy to give visitors a tour of the island; expect to pay around $50 for a 45-minute island tour.

FAST FACTS: Grand Turk

Area Code The area/country code for the TCI is **649.**

ATMs/ABMs **First Caribbean** (connected to the PLUS ABM network) has 24-hour ABM service at the main branch of its bank in Grand Turk (see "Banks," below). **Scotiabank** (connected to Cirrus) has an ATM at its main location on Grand Turk (open 24 hr. a day).

Banks Branches of the **First Caribbean International Bank** (© **649/946-2831**) and **Scotiabank** (© **649/946-4750**) are on Front Street in Cockburn Town.

Emergencies Call © **649/946-2299** if you need the police.

Hospitals/Medical Facilities **Grand Turk Hospital** is on Hospital Road in Grand Turk (© **649/946-2040**).

Internet Access You can access the Internet at the **Water's Edge restaurant** (Duke St; © © 649/946-1680), or try your hotel. Costs are typically around $10 an hour.

Language The official language is English.

Post Office The Grand Turk Post Office is located on Front Street in Cockburn Town. It's open Monday to Friday from 8am to 4pm.

Taxes The government collects a 10% occupancy tax, applicable to all hotels, guesthouses, and restaurants in the 40-island chain. Hotels often add a 10% to 15% service charge on top of the government tax.

WHERE TO STAY
HOTELS, RESORTS & INNS

Hotels add a 10% to 15% service charge, plus a 10% government occupancy tax, to the rates quoted below. Also keep in mind that many of the following resorts have a minimum-stay requirement during the winter high season.

Bohio Dive Resort ⟨⟩   New management has taken over what was previously the Pillory Beach Hotel, directly overlooking beautiful Pillory Beach—and the main feature is the hotel's in-house dive operation, with on-site PADI instructors and dive masters. Each of the 12 rooms and four suites, located in a separate building from the main section of the resort, has a private balcony with sea views. Chef Zev Beck is at the helm in the resort's gourmet restaurant, **Guanahani,** which serves breakfast, lunch, and dinner Friday to Tuesday; a bar menu, with burgers, fish, and conch, is offered all day long every day.

Front St. (P.O. Box 179), Grand Turk, Turks and Caicos, B.W.I. ⟨⟩ **649/946-2135.** Fax 649/946-1536. www.bohioresort.com. 16 units. Winter $155 double, $185 suite; off season $130 double, $150 suite. Dive rates include 2 morning boat dives. Children under 2 stay free in parent's room; children 3–12 $35 extra a night. AE, MC, V. **Amenities:** Restaurant; bar; outdoor pool; on-site dive instructors; dive shack; excursions; snorkeling; watersports; bikes; yoga. *In room:* A/C, TV, dataport, kitchenette (in suites), fridge, hair dryer, beverage maker, ceiling fan.

Grand Turk Inn ⟨⟩⟨⟩   These are the best accommodations in Grand Turk—it was recently even named best guesthouse in the entire TCI. Sisters Katrina Birt and Sandy Erb, veterans of the Key West inn scene, discovered the charms of Grand Turk and the excellent bones of this handsome Bermudan-style 150-year-old former Methodist manse, which they lovingly renovated. The five suites are spacious and ultracomfortable, with king- or queen-size beds dressed in soft linens; all have full kitchens and private bathrooms. The second-floor Pelican Suite can sleep up to four people. A big upper-floor sun deck overlooking the sea provides the perfect venue from which to watch humpback whales pass by in the winter.

Front St. (P.O. Box 9), Grand Turk, Turks and Caicos, B.W.I. ©/fax **649/946-2827**. www.grandturkinn.com. 5 units. Winter $300 double; summer $250 double. Rates include continental breakfast. AE, DISC, MC, V. No children under 16. **Amenities:** Bikes, sun deck, Wi-Fi. *In room:* A/C, TV/DVD, kitchen, hair dryer, safe, bathrobes, ceiling fan, Wi-Fi.

Island House *(Finds)*

On a breezy site overlooking North Creek, this inn is the creation of Colin Brooker, an English expat, and his Grand Turk–born wife, Lucy. The complex's architectural style evokes the Mediterranean, with rooms opening onto water views. The three studios and five one-bedroom suites are comfortable but nothing fancy; all have kitchens, bathrooms with tub and shower, and balconies with sumptuous views overlooking the water and the well-planted gardens. It's not on the beach, but you can easily get there by gas-powered golf cart or one of the vehicles provided for guests—either a van or a pickup truck. The idyllic spot here is a pool set against a backdrop of tropical vegetation. Activities such as fishing and scuba diving can be arranged. The hotel offers its own dock on North Creek, featuring sailing, canoeing, and windsurfing.

Lighthouse Rd. (P.O. Box 36), Grand Turk, Turks and Caicos, B.W.I. © **649/946-1519**. Fax 649/946-2646. www.islandhouse-tci.com. 8 units. Winter (2-night package) $187–$220 per person nondiver, $258–$290 per person diver; off season (2-night package) $170–$204 per person nondiver, $240–$274 per person diver. Dive rates include 2 morning boat dives. Children under 12 stay free in parent's room. Rates include personal use of pickup truck or golf cart and round-trip airport transfers. AE, MC, V. **Amenities:** Outdoor freshwater pool; babysitting; coin-operated laundry; barbecue grill; dock; fishing; sailing; snorkeling; windsurfing; bikes. *In room:* A/C, TV, dataport, kitchen, fridge, hair dryer, safe, beverage maker, ceiling fan.

Manta House

You can't ask for a better location than that enjoyed by this funky little B&B, a favorite of divers. The guesthouse features three pleasant B&B rooms (sharing one bathroom), and the two sprawling bungalows have living rooms and private bathrooms. The North Bungalow has a full kitchen and two private patios.

Duke St. (P.O. Box 222), Grand Turk, Turks & Caicos, B.W.I. © **649/946-1111**. www. grandturk-mantahouse.com. 5 units. Winter $995–$1,300 bungalow, $78 double; off season $795–$1,100 bungalow, $73 double. Dive packages $60 per person per day. Rates include continental breakfast. MC, V. **Amenities:** Restaurant; bar; fridge. *In room:* A/C, kitchen (in North Bungalow).

Osprey Beach Hotel *(Kids)*

This landmark hotel has a lovely white-sand-beach setting that offers good swimming and snorkeling. Twenty-seven bedrooms occupy modern two-story town houses, each with oceanfront verandas, but 12 more units are

Raking & Making Salt

The large, shallow, stone-bordered ponds in the middle of Grand Turk are not just nesting sites for flamingos and other brilliant birds: They are **salinas,** abandoned artifacts of the salt industry, which ruled the Grand Turk and Salt Cay economies for 300 years. The salt industry began with seasonal salt-rakers coming to the TCI from Bermuda in the late 1600s and lasted until commercial exploitation of the salinas ended in the 1960s. Grand Turk and Salt Cay, the original salt-producing islands, have several natural, shallow, inland depressions (salinas) that filled with salt water directly from the sea or percolated up from underlying rock. Bermudians improved the natural salinas, making them into rock-bordered salt pans or ponds. Salt was made by letting seawater into the salinas through sluice gates located at the beach. Water was concentrated by evaporation in one pond, then concentrated again in a second. The slushy brine was then let into smaller drying pans, where the salt crystallized. The cycle took about 90 days from start to finish, but "crops" for each set of pans were spaced by the individual stages into 20- to 30-day periods. Workers raked the crystallized salt into piles and shoveled it into wheelbarrows. Raking salt under the midday sun was an incredibly labor-intensive business, and many who worked the salt (including a number of slaves) were felled by the brutal conditions.

Who used all this salt? From the time of the first European settlements in North America to the middle of the 1800s, salt was a critical food-preservation item. The United States was dependent upon salt imports to some degree until almost the end of the 19th century. The relative importance of the Turks Islands, however, dwindled as the demand for salt expanded. Dwarfed by the demand and other producers and unable to expand pond acreage, mechanize loading, or achieve economies of scale, the salt industry in the Turks Islands finally collapsed in the 1960s after 300 years of production.

—*Courtesy of the Turks & Caicos National Museum*

located in the older building across the street, home to the **Courtyard Café,** which serves breakfast and lunch. Some rooms have kitchenettes, but all contain ceiling fans and fridges plus small bathrooms with tub/shower combinations. (Rooms on the upper floors are larger and have higher ceilings.) Ask for one of the handsomely renovated rooms shown on the website; alas, our room could have used some refreshing, particularly the motel-style bathroom. Dinner is served at the **Birdcage Bar & Restaurant;** on Sunday and Wednesday nights, the whole of Duke Street and beyond seems to congregate for the **poolside barbecue buffet** ($14–$26) and the toe-tapping ripsaw music of "dive-master troubadour" Mitch Rolling and the High Tide.

Duke St. (P.O. Box 216), Grand Turk, Turks and Caicos, B.W.I. ⓒ **649/946-2666.** Fax 649/946-2817. www.ospreybeachhotel.com. 39 units. $323–$409 per person double occupancy for 3-night stay; courtyard rooms (in Atrium) $208–$248 per person double occupancy for 3-night stay. Children under 12 stay free in parent's room. Dive packages available. AE, MC, V. **Amenities:** Restaurant/cafe; bar; outdoor pool; laundry service; rooms for those w/limited mobility. *In room:* A/C, TV, dataport, kitchenette (in some), fridge, ceiling fan.

The Salt Raker Inn   Once the home of a shipwright who emigrated here from Bermuda, this inn—one of the most historic on the islands—dates from the early 1800s. Today it's been converted into a small inn with a well-recommended restaurant (see Secret Garden, below) and a genial owner. The hotel stands right across the street from a good beach of golden sands. The Salt Raker has a certain rough-hewn charm, and the location can't be beat, but rooms are serviceable at best, especially the downstairs units. The best rooms by far are the upstairs suites, which share a lovely, breezy balcony with hammocks and great sea views.

1 Duke St., Grand Turk, Turks & Caicos, B.W.I. ⓒ **649/946-2260.** Fax 649/946-2263. www.saltraker.com. 13 units. Winter $110–$119 double, $149 suite; off season $95–$109 double, $135 suite. MC, V. **Amenities:** Restaurant; room service (daily 7:30am–9:30pm); babysitting; laundry service. *In room:* A/C, TV, beverage maker (in suites).

VILLAS

A growing number of visitors—families in particular—are looking to rent villas or apartments on Grand Turk. The four two-story modern town-house units of **Arches of Grand Turk Island** (Lighthouse Rd.; ⓒ **649/946-2941;** www.grandturkarches.com; winter $180–$300 per night, $1,160–$2,000 per week; off season $160–$280 per night, $1,020–$1,860 per week) are located on the

Dining in Margaritaville

At press time **Jimmy Buffett's Margaritaville** had just opened in the Grand Turk Cruise Center. It's an impressive sight: the largest stand-alone Margaritaville in the entire Caribbean. The colorful, vintage-Bermudan–style restaurant is bordered by a large, lagoon-like pool with a swim-up bar, slide, and infinity edge. Currently the cruise center is only open on those days when ships come in (2–3 days a week), but that's soon to change. Please contact the cruise center at © **649/ 946-1040** for information about the restaurant hours and opening times.

island's North Ridge. Each unit has two bedrooms, two bathrooms, and a full kitchen, and the complex has a nice freshwater swimming pool.

Aqua House (Close Haul Rd.; contactus@aquahouse.tc; www. aquahouse.biz; $1,500–$1,600 per week) has two oceanfront condominiums, each with two bedrooms, two bathrooms, balconies with views, and bikes.

DINING

Fairly new at press time but highly recommended for its authentic island cuisine is **A Taste of the Island** (West St.; © 649/946-2112). Also recommended for its stellar platters of fried chicken (no less than the *Washington Post* raved about it) is the **Poop Deck,** a wooden shack on Front Street (no phone). Don't miss the **Sunday-night poolside barbecues** at the **Birdcage,** in the Osprey Beach Hotel on Duke Street. The restaurant is also open for dinner (© 649/946-2666).

You may not want to kill time at the Grand Turk airport—but given certain local airlines' island-time mentality, you may be forced to. Here's a silver lining, however: the airport restaurant. The **Cockpit Lounge** has surprisingly good island food (it feeds a lot of government officials traveling to and from Cockburn Town), including cracked conch, fish and fries, garlic shrimp, and more (© 649/946-1095; open Mon–Sat 6am–9pm, Sun 6am–8:30pm; main courses $10–$20, sandwiches and burgers $4–$9, salads $5–$15). The restaurant also offers Internet access.

The Courtyard Café OMELETS/SANDWICHES Someone in the kitchen is an omelet master—they're cooked to perfection with just the right amount of filler. This popular breakfast and lunch spot also serves homemade waffles, sandwiches, and salads.

1 Duke St. ✆ **649/946-2260.** Reservations recommended in winter. Breakfast $5–$12; lunch specials $9–$18; dinner $12–$30. MC, V. Daily 7:30am–9:30pm

The Sandbar CARIBBEAN/BURGERS   This little open-air bar/ restaurant is set above the beach, with a blond-wood deck and seating overlooking the sea. It's a casual, friendly watering hole, with local color provided by a dog or two lying in the cool sand. It's owned by two energetic Canadian sisters, Tonya and Katya, who also run the Manta House B&B (see above) across the street, and it's a social hub for locals and visitors alike. The menu is much more interesting than a beach bar's needs to be, with lobster quesadilla, cracked conch, shrimp and chips, and very respectable burgers.

Duke St. ✆ **649/946-1111.** Main courses $11–$15. MC, V. Daily noon–late.

Secret Garden SEAFOOD/CARIBBEAN   Tucked in the covered backyard garden of The Salt Raker Inn (see above), this casual eatery is an island favorite. Lunch specials are tasty and include grouper sandwich, barbecued chicken, and even a hearty spaghetti Bolognese. In the evening you can start with conch bites and settle on an entree of grouper, seafood pasta, garlic shrimp, cracked conch, or curry goat, with a side of peas and rice, of course.

1 Duke St. ✆ **649/946-2260.** Reservations recommended in winter. English breakfast $5–$12; lunch specials $9–$18; dinner $12–$21. MC, V. Daily 7:30–10am, noon–2:30pm, and 7–9:30pm.

ⓘTips **Shopping for Self-Catering**

Many resorts and rented villas have full kitchens for **self-catering.** You can get all your basic provisions (food, drinks, snacks, toiletries, even fishing gear) at **Cee's Superstore** (Pond Rd.; ✆ **649/946-2995**). **Dot's Food Fair** (Hospital Rd., ✆ **649/ 946-2324**), located in the old town center, also offers a grocery/basic provisions store as well as a boutique with toiletries, books, clothes, you name it. Buy **fresh fish** straight off the dock on Front Street when fishermen come in at the end of the day. Liquor, beer, and wine can be bought at any grocery or convenience store (except on Sun) or at **Dot's Liquors** (yes, the very same Dot of Dot's Food Fair), across from the Red Salina on Pond Street.

Water's Edge BAHAMIAN/AMERICAN   Set directly over the beach, close to the center of town, this popular watering hole (happy hour sees a lot of sun-blasted divers) was changing management at press time, so we'll have to see how the new version fares. Come here for amazing views of the sea, an engaging informality, and free Internet access. Expect standard conch, fish, and chicken dishes—and hopefully, faster service.

Duke St. 𝒞 **649/946-1680.** Main courses $13–$30. MC, V. Daily 11am–11pm.

SCUBA DIVING & SNORKELING 𝔯𝔯𝔯

Some of the finest **scuba diving** in the archipelago is around Grand Turk—in fact, a breathtakingly short .8km to 1.6km (½–1 mile) offshore (a 5- to 10-min. boat ride away). The action is at the **"Wall,"** where the western edges of the island (and its necklace of coral reef) plunge dramatically 2,134m (7,000 ft.) into deep water, actually the leeward side of the Turks Island Passage (also known as the Columbus Passage), which lies between the Turks Islands and the Caicos Islands. Scuba divers flock here to enjoy panoramic wall dives on the vertical sides of the reefs. The diving sites of the Wall have colorful names like Coral Garden, the Aquarium, the Library, and even McDonald's (for its—what else?—coral arch). Near Governor's Beach (and just onshore, the governor's mansion at Waterloo) is a site called Chief Ministers. You'll see all manner of marine life, from giant manta rays and Nassau groupers to big, voluptuous formations of coral and sponges. You'll even see humpback whales as they migrate south through the Turks Island Passage in the winter.

"See" is the operative word in Grand Turk diving: The visibility can exceed 30m (100 ft.). And you don't have to go deep to encounter impressive marine life—active reef zones begin here at depths of just 9m (30 ft.)—meaning you'll enjoy productive dives in better light and using better air production. The proximity of great diving to the docks also means you don't have to spend hours getting to and from your dives—after an afternoon dive you can be back on land in plenty of time for happy hour.

You can also enjoy one of the underwater world's great experiences: a **night dive** on the Wall, where, due to bioluminescence, the colors of the day become the phosphorescent illumination of the night.

Snorkeling is good right off many Grand Turk beaches, including **Governor's Beach, White Sands Beach,** and **Pillory Beach** (in front of the Bohio Dive Resort). Many dive operators also offer snorkeling trips out to the reef, or, when space allows, take snorkelers out on dive boats, where you will snorkel in water depths of approximately 8m (25 ft.). The dive shops discussed below all rent snorkel gear.

One extremely popular snorkeling trip is to uninhabited **Gibbs Cay,** where you can not only snorkel in clear turquoise shallows but hand-feed and touch docile stingrays.

DIVE OPERATORS

The owners and operators of the following dive companies are experienced divers on the island, and they know where to find marine life in a kaleidoscope of colors. They work with novices—offering good beginning courses and training—as well as experienced divers of all skill levels. Rates below are per person.

Blue Water Divers, on Front Street (©/fax **649/946-1226;** www.grandturkscuba.com), offers single dives, PADI registration, and dive packages, and even runs trips to Salt Cay. These people are top-rate and will tell you many facts and legends about diving in their country (like the fact that the highest mountain in the Turks & Caicos is 2,400m/7,872 ft. tall, but only the top 42m/138 ft. are above sea level!). A single-tank dive costs $45, with a two-tank dive going for $80; a night dive costs $50. Trips to Salt Cay and Gibbs Cay cost $60. Full PADI certification is $400. (Mitch Rolling, the Blue Water Divers dive master, is also the guitarist who plays at the Osprey Beach Hotel on Sun and Wed barbecue nights with the ripsaw band High Tide.)

Cecil Ingham's Sea Eye Diving, on Duke Street (© **649/946-1407;** www.seaeyediving.com), is convenient to most hotels in town. It offers two-tank morning dives at $65 to $75. An afternoon single-tank dive costs $45, and a single-tank night dive goes for $50. Rental equipment is also available. NAUI and PADI courses at all levels are offered. A full-certification course goes for $400, including training equipment and boat checkout dives. Dive packages that include accommodations can be arranged at a hotel of your choice. Snorkeling and cay trips are available for nondivers.

Oasis Divers, on Duke Street (© **649/946-1128;** www.oasis divers.com), offers complete dive-master services, with dive adventures along the Wall, night dives, trips to Gibbs Cay, snorkeling trips, trips to Salt Cay, and dive/accommodations packages. A morning two-tank dive costs $86; a night dive is $50. An instruction course and dive from your resort is $110; a trip to Salt Cay is $50 and a trip to Gibbs Cay is $55.

EXPLORING THE ISLAND

People go to Grand Turk mainly to swim, snorkel, dive, or do nothing but soak up the sun. Other activities include bird-watching, horseback riding, heritage walks, and golf. You might also take a pleasant bike ride to the Northwest Point to see the newly sand-blasted cast-iron **Grand Turk Lighthouse,** which was brought in pieces from the United Kingdom, where it had been constructed in 1852. Its old lens is on display in the Turks & Caicos National Museum.

Grand Turk Cruise Center   This is an impressive sight indeed—a 5.7-hectare (14-acre) cruise-ship terminal designed by the folks at Carnival Cruise Lines to resemble a colorful Bermudan-style village out of the early 19th century, much like Cockburn Town might have looked in the early 1800s. The center is planted smack dab on Governor's Beach, with a 172m-long (565-ft.) main pier, hundreds of deck chairs along the beach, a huge Jimmy Buffet's Margaritaville (with lagoonlike pool), a main building with four vintage-style chimneys prominently on view, and shops designed to resemble the quaint wooden "salt houses" of the salt era—many of which are locally owned and sell island crafts and gifts. It all lies mute and still until the arrival of a 2,000-passenger ship (currently 3 days a week on average), which shows up on the empty horizon just as the sun comes up—a watery behemoth that gets eye-poppingly bigger as it approaches this tiny island. A miniature train takes arriving cruise passengers to Governor's Beach, or they can choose one of the myriad activities created for them: seeing Cockburn Town by beach buggy, horse-drawn carriage, moped, or shuttle taxi. Or they can participate in a shore excursion (scuba diving, snorkeling, horseback riding) available through local tour operators and purchased through the cruise line.

Waterloo Rd. ⓒ **649/946-1040.** www.grandturkcc.com.

Turks & Caicos National Museum ⓖⓖ   This is the country's first (and only) museum. It occupies a 150-year-old residence, Guinep House, originally built by Bermudan wreckers from timbers they salvaged from ships that crashed on nearby reefs. Today about half of its display areas are devoted to the remains of the most complete archaeological excavation ever performed in the West Indies, the wreck of a Spanish caravel (sailing ship) that sank in shallow water sometime before 1513. Used to transport local Lucayans who had been enslaved, the boat was designed solely for exploration purposes and is similar to vessels built in Spain and Portugal during the 1400s.

Treasure hunters found the wreck and announced that it was Columbus's *Pinta,* in order to attract financial backers for their salvage—to guarantee a value to the otherwise-valueless iron artifacts, in case there proved to be no gold onboard. There is no proof, however, that the *Pinta* ever came back to the New World after returning to Spain from the first voyage. Researchers from the Institute of Nautical Archaeology at Texas A&M University began excavations in 1982, although staff members never assumed that the wreck was the *Pinta.* Today the remains are referred to simply as the Wreck of Molasses Reef.

Although only 2% of the hull now remains intact, the exhibits contain a rich legacy of the everyday (nonbiodegradable) objects used by the crews and officers.

The remainder of the museum is devoted to exhibits about the island's salt industries, its plantation economy, the pre-Columbian inhabitants of the island, and its natural history. The natural-history exhibit features a 2m×6m (6½×20-ft.), three-dimensional reproduction of a section of the Grand Turk Wall, the famous vertical reef. You'll also find displays on the geology of the islands and information on the reef and coral growth.

Guinep House, Front St., Cockburn Town, Grand Turk. ℭ 649/946-2160. www.tc museum.org. Admission $5 nonresidents, free for full-time island residents. Mon–Tues and Thurs–Fri 9am–4pm; Wed 9am–5pm; Sat 9am–1pm.

Waterloo Golf Club   Former TCI governor John Kelly loved golf so much he designed and actually helped build this 9-hole course on the grounds of the governor's mansion (Waterloo) and office—it was opened in 1998. Now anyone can play here; call to reserve your tee time.

Waterloo Rd. ℭ 649/946-2308. Greens fees $25 per day.

GRAND TURK AFTER DARK

Nookie Hill Club, Nookie Hill (no phone), offers dancing and late-night drinking. At the previously recommended **Osprey Beach Hotel,** on Duke Street (ℭ 649/946-2666), Wednesday and Sunday barbecues feature music by Mitch Rolling and the High Tide (see below).

Rippin' Ripsaw

Attend the poolside barbecue at the Osprey Beach Hotel, held every Sunday and Wednesday night, and you'll find yourself enjoying more than the excellent buffet of local dishes. Mitch Rolling and the High Tide play music with a uniquely infectious beat that can't help but get your toes tapping (or even, with the encouragement of a few Turk's Head lagers, get up and dance). That beat comes partly from the goatskin drum and maracas being played alongside the guitar-strumming Mitch (dive master for the Blue Water Divers outfit by day); but the sound that crawls right into your nervous system comes from the guy holding that strange-but-familiar-looking piece of metal against his thigh and drawing another familiar-looking implement across it. He's playing a handsaw by scraping its teeth vigorously with the shaft of a long-handled screwdriver (the blade of an old knife can also be used). The result is a wonderful, rasping sound that turns any song, from a pop standard to traditional island music, into a rocking, calypso-style dance tune.

Ripsaw music, also known as "rake and scrape," is the national music of Turks & Caicos, and it can be heard across the archipelago. Playing a ripsaw is harder than it looks: Neophytes find their arms and wrists tiring after just a few minutes, but with practice, ripsaw players learn to sustain their art for a full 2- or 3-hour show. The origins of ripsaw are unclear. Some say the art form was brought back to the islands by Belongers who fell in love with a similar style of music played in Haiti and the Dominican Republic and used locally available tools to re-create the rhythms here. Others surmise that the instrumental style was brought here by slaves of Loyalists fleeing the American Revolution. Whatever its roots, it's a style you're sure to fall in love with, too.

2 Salt Cay ★★

When they *really* want to relax, the stressed-out denizens of sleepy Grand Turk head here, to Salt Cay (pop. 60), for a sundowner, perhaps, at the Green Flash or the Coral Bar & Grill. As one Grand Turker put it: "Salt Cay has two speeds: slow and stop."

Salt Cay

ATTRACTIONS ●
White House **3**

ACCOMMODATIONS ■
Pirate's Hideaway **1**
Tradewinds Guest Suites **4**
Windmills Plantation **8**

DINING ◆
Coral Reef **6**
Green Flash **5**
Island Thyme Bistro **7**
Pat's Place **2**

Salt Cay's slogan is "The Land that Time Forgot," and if you arrive by air on the bumpy island airstrip—whose one-room airport resembles a Wild West storefront, complete with hitching post—you'll get the idea. You may feel slightly panicked at first, particularly after absorbing the lay of the land on the fly-in: the tiny (2.6 sq. km/1 sq. mile), rural landscape, dotted with abandoned salinas and old windmills, sunbaked remnants of the Bermudian salt-rakers' heyday on the island in the early 19th century, and the occasional donkey ambling down a dirt road. If you spot a car at all, it's probably Nathan Smith picking you up at the airport.

It's a wonder you don't head home on the next flight.

But don't. Give this, the southernmost cay of the Turks Islands, a couple of days, at the very least. Grab a snorkel and flippers and dip into the sea right off the beach. Have a lively lunch at Island Thyme Bistro and gaze at the Haitian art papering the walls. Find a message in a bottle lying on the beach. Have a sunset drink at the Green Flash as you stare out at the horizon for the green flash. Swim with whales (or stingrays if you prefer). Rent a golf cart from Nathan Smith, buy groceries from Nathan Smith, and get a taxi ride from Nathan Smith. Or just find yourself a hammock or a prime spot on the sugary-sand beach and enjoy one of the most tranquil places you'll ever experience.

ESSENTIALS
VISITOR INFORMATION

Salt Cay has its own very informative website (**www.saltcay.org**), which has a business directory—with listings of accommodations, restaurants, grocery stores, watersports operators, golf-cart rentals, and the like—a map of the island, history, and much more.

Salt Cay has three grocery/convenience stores: **Smith's Shopping Center, Nettie's Store,** and **Pat's Store.** Nettie Talbot, born and bred on Salt Cay, sells fresh-baked bread out of her store

GETTING TO SALT CAY

Only two airlines have planes small enough to land and take off from the tiny runway at the Salt Cay airport, but at press time the government had earmarked considerable funds to lengthen and resurface the airstrip and upgrade South Dock; work was to begin immediately and may be completed by the time this guide is in the stores—once finished, airlines like SkyKing (see contact information earlier in this chapter) can deliver visitors to this delightful

Porter Williams's Favorite TCI Experiences

Porter Williams, the owner of Island Thyme Bistro and tireless promoter of all things Salt Cay, first came to the island in the mid-1990s. It was during his first visit to Salt Cay, Porter says, that he became part and parcel of the community. After years of being guests, he and his wife decided that they wanted their children to grow up island-style. They bought a historic structure, and, with the help of local craftsmen, created Island Thyme Bistro. Since then, Porter has danced with Miss Alice at the Senior Citizen's Ball, was Santa at the annual children's Christmas Party, learned to make johnnycakes from Miss Nettie, and dived with manta rays. Here are Porter Williams's favorite TCI experiences:

- eating chicken wings at the **Green Flash Cafe** (Deane's Dock area; (C) 649/946-6904; www.saltcaytours.net) on Wednesday night
- attending glowworm parties
- snorkeling for conch and swimming with whales
- sampling cracked conch at **Pat's Place** (p. 143)
- enjoying a margarita at the **Coral Reef Bar & Grill** (Deane's Dock area; (C) 649/946-6940)
- dining at the **Windmills Plantation** (p. 142)
- walking on a deserted beach
- exploring and looking for treasure
- visiting with old and new friends
- looking at the stars
- enjoying the ultimate freedom of living in a place where everyone is accepted and becomes part of the community

island. Currently, however, only **Air Turks & Caicos** ((C) **649/941-5481** or 649/946-6940, -6906 on Salt Cay; www.airturksandcaicos.com) and **Global Airways** charters ((C) **649/941-3222;** www.global airways.tc) fly to Salt Cay.

Air Turks & Caicos offers regularly scheduled flights daily between Provo and Grand Turk (see above), and then three flights a day from Grand Turk to Salt Cay; the Grand Turk–Salt Cay leg takes under 10 minutes and costs $50 round-trip. The one daily flight from Provo to Salt Cay takes 30 minutes and costs $165.

Contact Global for schedules, which can change daily.

A government-subsidized **ferry** runs between Grand Turk and Salt Cay, weather permitting, every Wednesday and Friday (leaving from South Dock—the island's *only* dock, by the way—at Salt Cay at 7:30am and returning at 2:30pm). The trip takes an hour and costs $12. You can also hire a **private-boat operator** to take you between Salt Cay and Grand Turk (as long as the seas aren't too rough). Contact Nathan Smith (see below) or hire a boat charter with **Salt Cay Adventure Tours** (© **649/946-6909;** www.saltcay tours.com). **Cruise-ship passengers** who arrive in Grand Turk can also contact Salt Cay Adventures to arrange day trips to Salt Cay.

GETTING AROUND SALT CAY

No one needs a car to get around Salt Cay, which has more donkeys than cars to begin with; it's the perfect place for getting around on foot, by bike, or by golf cart. **Nathan Smith,** the "unofficial mayor of Salt Cay," not only offers taxi service from the airport but rents golf carts and bikes (and offers tours of all kinds, including snorkeling and troll fishing for tuna). Contact **Smith's Golf-Cart & Bike Rental,** located next to the Salt Cay Divers dive shop (© **649/946-6928** or cellphone 649/231-4856; two-seater golf-carts $50/day, $280/week; four-seaters $60/day, $350/week; bikes $10/day; credit cards accepted).

WHERE TO STAY IN SALT CAY

Salt Cay has only a handful of inn-style lodgings, and in 2006 it lost a longtime favorite: The historic **Mount Pleasant Guest House** has been sold and is now a private residence.

The island has a number of **villas and cottages to rent.** For an updated directory of these, go to **www.saltcay.org**.

Pirate's Hideaway This little guesthouse offers two full-service suites and Blackbeard's Quarters, a four-bedroom house. It has the only freshwater pool on the island and a tropical garden. On-site is the Salt Cay Smugglers Tavern, where you can drink a cool beer and munch on the likes of snapper or Caribbean chicken. The guesthouse is not on the beach but just a block away.

Victoria St., Salt Cay, Turks and Caicos, B.W.I. ©/fax **649/946-6909.** www.pirates hideaway.com. 3 units. Double $165–$175. Blackbeard's Quarters $400 per night. Dive packages available. MC, V. **Amenities:** Bistro/bar; freshwater pool. *In room:* A/C, kitchenette (Blackbeard's Quarters only), ceiling fan.

Tradewinds Guest Suites Tradewinds offers five one-bedroom self-catering suites steps away from a lovely beach shaded by casuarina trees. Each suite has a kitchen or kitchenette, bedroom, living room with a sofa bed, private bathroom, and a screened porch. You can ask the staff to stock food for your arrival, or choose an all-inclusive meal and dive package.

Victoria St., Salt Cay, Turks and Caicos, B.W.I. ℂ **649/946-6906.** Fax 649/946-6940. www.tradewinds.tc. 5 units. Winter $145–$175 double; off season $115–$129 double. Weekly rates available. Ask about meal and dive packages. MC, V. **Amenities:** Bikes; barbecue grills; hammocks. *In room:* A/C, kitchen/kitchenette, fridge, ceiling fan.

Windmills Plantation 𝒜𝒜   If you like your luxury lodgings with a distinctly boho flavor and more than a touch of whimsy, head here, to Salt Cay's only high-end resort. The roofs of the inn's fanciful structures are splashed in bright blues, reds, and yellows; the bar's decorations are flotsam and jetsam picked up from the Salt Cay beaches. Windmills is a hedonistic delight, from the big rooms with big four-posters and fall-out-of-your-bed snorkeling right off the beach to the sundowners in the burnt-orange twilight and the elegant (but barefoot) candlelit dinners at night. The life-is-a-party atmosphere is contagious, but so is the luxuriant languor—the hammock and sun-kissed air await you. The building of this resort in 1980 is the topic of a fascinating book, *The Carnival Never Got Started,* by the creator himself, Guy Lovelace.

Salt Cay, Turks and Caicos, B.W.I. ℂ **649/946-6962.** Fax 649/946-6930. www. windmillsplantation.com. 8 units. Double $655–$685. Rates include all meals. No children. AE, MC, V. **Amenities:** Restaurant; bar; outdoor saltwater pool; game room; bikes; snorkeling. *In room:* A/C, ceiling fan, private plunge pools (in some), no phone.

WHERE TO DINE IN SALT CAY

Nonguests can reserve a **gourmet dinner** 𝒜 at the Windmills Plantation. The prix-fixe meals include soup, appetizer, entree, and dessert ($60 per person, drinks extra; reservations required).

Island Thyme Bistro CARIBBEAN/INTERNATIONAL 𝒜   If this is the nerve center of Salt Cay, then its ebullient owner, Porter Williams, is its commander. The Island Thyme is more than just a good place to eat—it's the local bank, the Internet access center, and party central. Where else can you sip a cool Cuba Libre while cheering on a hermit crab race? Where else can you dine out on seared rare sirloin and grilled lobster, smoke a fine Cuban cigar, and then walk home in your bare feet? Porter Williams brings together the widely disparate passions of his life in this delightful restaurant, and visitors are the better for it. Island Thyme is open for breakfast, lunch, and dinner and has a lively bar scene—ask about the Wolf shooter, but sign over everything you own to a trusted family member before partaking. At night, sample such delicacies as coconut shrimp, almond-crusted snapper, duck breast, or even sushi. See you at Wednesday Wing Night!

Salt Cay. ©/fax **649/946-6977**. Main courses $15–$33. MC, V. Daily 7–9am, noon–2pm, and 6:30–9pm. Closed 1 day a week;2 months a year (generally May–July).

Pat's Place ✪ ISLAND   Pat Simmons is a retired schoolteacher (she taught for 28 years in the Salt Cay school system) who now runs this modest eatery out of her home, on a latticed screened-in patio with yellow walls, green trim, and bright-colored tablecloths. Call ahead to say you're coming, give Pat your order, and when you arrive, you'll be treated to delicious island food served family-style. Choose from steamed or fried fish, curry conch, barbecued chicken, peas and rice, greens, and more. Beer and wine are available.

Historic South District. © **649/946-6919**. Reservations required for all meals. $15 per person dinner without beer or wine. No credit cards. Daily 7:30am–9:30pm

EXPLORING SALT CAY

Aside from the salinas, some interesting architecture remains from the salt-raking days of the early 19th century. The 1834 stone-and-stucco **White House** was the home of a Bermudian salt-raker; the downstairs is a salt warehouse (tour by appointment only).

   Salt Cay Adventure Tours (© **649/946-6909;** www.saltcaytours. com) is an all-purpose watersports activities operator. They can arrange scuba-diving trips (for a fully equipped PADI dive shop, see **Salt Cay Divers,** below), guide you on snorkeling, whale-watching, or snorkeling adventures, rent out bikes and kayaks, and will do island-history and art tours. **Cruise-ship passengers** who arrive in Grand Turk can also contact Salt Cay Adventures to arrange day trips to Salt Cay.

SCUBA DIVING

Divers can explore the wreck of the **HMS *Endymion*** ✪ off Salt Cay, which went down in a storm in 1790. Two centuries later, Brian Sheedy, a local diver and inn operator, discovered the wreck. Today, while the reef has reclaimed the hull and all else that was biodegradable, divers can still get a close-up look at its 18 coral- and sponge-encrusted cannons and nine huge anchors lying about. Resting in just 12m (40 ft.) of water, it's one of the region's most popular snorkel and dive sites.

Diving Salt Cay's Walls

The Northwest Wall, Kelly's Folly, and Turtle Garden offer wall diving at its finest—and all of these dive sites are 5 to 10 minutes from the Salt Cay dock. Huge gorgonians, soft coral, and sponges form a backdrop for a family of spotted eagle rays, turtles, pelagics, and dolphins. A green moray eel whose head is at least .3m high (1 ft.), his huge body and tail wrapped in and out of a rock formation, can often be seen at Northwest Wall and Rockery. Divers can observe conch working their way up a timeworn trail on the wall. Night-dive with fluorescent strings of pearls threading their way through the water, sleeping turtles, slipper lobsters, huge crabs, nurse sharks, and a seasonal array of other night critters.

—*Michele Belanger-McNair and Debbie Been,*
Salt Cay Divers

A fully equipped PADI dive shop with instruction at every level, **Salt Cay Divers** (② **649/946-6906;** www.saltcaydivers.tc) offers scuba divers small groups and personalized service. Children can learn to dive in the Bubble Maker program while Mom and Dad get their certification or advanced rating. Carolina skiffs are able to get up close to prime reefs and dive sites, and a 9.8m (32-ft.) V-hull is used for longer, smoother rides to other islands and cays. Salt Cay Divers regularly dives South Caicos's reefs as well as Grand Turk's dive sites.

SNORKELING

As good as the diving is on Salt Cay, it may be an even better snorkeling destination; the island, in fact, has some of the best snorkeling in the TCI, and you can do most of it right off the beaches. The **Bluff, Point Pleasant,** and **Aquarium** sites offer opportunities to watch squid, tarpon, barracuda, and colorful coral heads and fans. **Queen's Beach,** on the north shore, is another great spot to see lots of brilliantly hued fish.

Day trips to **Great Sand Cay,** an uninhabited national park, allow picnickers to snorkel, swim, view iguanas and tide pools, and bird-watch. Other uninhabited islands can be visited, such as **Gibbs**

Cay, where you can snorkel with stingrays. At **Whale Island** you can walk off the beach with snorkel and mask to see parrotfish and stingrays. Day trips to these cays (as well as overnight trips to Great Sand Cay) can be arranged through Salt Cay Divers (see above).

WHALE-WATCHING

Between January and April, **humpback whales** come here to play as they travel the 2,134m (7,000-ft.) trench of the Columbus Passage to the Silver Banks to mate and calf. Visitors can watch their antics from shore, boat out among them, or strap on dive or snorkeling equipment and go below. Salt Cay is one of the last places in the world you can actually get in the water and swim with these impressive creatures. Salt Cay Divers does what is called "soft water encounters." As Debbie Been of Salt Cay Divers explains it: "We gently slide into the water after ensuring that the whales are not frightened by our presence. Then the whales actually swim toward you. We ask that you not get too close, but believe me, those whales know exactly where you are—and if they wanted to hurt you, they would, but they are truly gentle creatures. We snorkel for a few minutes and watch their graceful bodies underwater. The usual encounter only lasts a few minutes, but it's the thrill of a lifetime."

Index

See also Accommodations and Restaurant indexes below.

ACCOMMODATIONS

Explore over 3,500 destinations.

TOKYO — 7766 miles
LONDON — 3818 miles
TORONTO — 4682 miles
SYDNEY — 5087 miles
NEW YORK — 4947 miles
LOS ANGELES — 2556 miles
HONG KONG — 5638 miles

FROMMER'S® COMPLETE TRAVEL GUIDES

FROMMER'S® DAY BY DAY GUIDES

PAULINE FROMMER'S GUIDES! SEE MORE. SPEND LESS.

FROMMER'S® PORTABLE GUIDES

FROMMER'S® CRUISE GUIDES

Alaska Cruises & Ports of Call

Cruises & Ports of Call

European Cruises & Ports of Call

FROMMER'S® NATIONAL PARK GUIDES

Algonquin Provincial Park
Banff & Jasper
Grand Canyon

National Parks of the American West
Rocky Mountain
Yellowstone & Grand Teton

Yosemite and Sequoia & Kings
  Canyon
Zion & Bryce Canyon

FROMMER'S® MEMORABLE WALKS

London
New York

Paris
Rome

San Francisco

FROMMER'S® WITH KIDS GUIDES

Chicago
Hawaii
Las Vegas
London

National Parks
New York City
San Francisco

Toronto
Walt Disney World® & Orlando
Washington, D.C.

SUZY GERSHMAN'S BORN TO SHOP GUIDES

France
Hong Kong, Shanghai & Beijing
Italy

London
New York

Paris
San Francisco

FROMMER'S® IRREVERENT GUIDES

Amsterdam
Boston
Chicago
Las Vegas

London
Los Angeles
Manhattan
Paris

Rome
San Francisco
Walt Disney World®
Washington, D.C.

FROMMER'S® BEST-LOVED DRIVING TOURS

Austria
Britain
California
France

Germany
Ireland
Italy
New England

Northern Italy
Scotland
Spain
Tuscany & Umbria

THE UNOFFICIAL GUIDES®

Adventure Travel in Alaska
Beyond Disney
California with Kids
Central Italy
Chicago
Cruises
Disneyland®
England
Florida
Florida with Kids

Hawaii
Ireland
Las Vegas
London
Maui
Mexico's Best Beach Resorts
Mini Mickey
New Orleans
New York City

Paris
San Francisco
South Florida including Miami &
  the Keys
Walt Disney World®
Walt Disney World® for
  Grown-ups
Walt Disney World® with Kids
Washington, D.C.

SPECIAL-INTEREST TITLES

Athens Past & Present
Best Places to Raise Your Family
Cities Ranked & Rated
500 Places to Take Your Kids Before They Grow Up
Frommer's Best Day Trips from London
Frommer's Best RV & Tent Campgrounds
  in the U.S.A.

Frommer's Exploring America by RV
Frommer's NYC Free & Dirt Cheap
Frommer's Road Atlas Europe
Frommer's Road Atlas Ireland
Great Escapes From NYC Without Wheels
Retirement Places Rated

FROMMER'S® PHRASEFINDER DICTIONARY GUIDES

French

Italian

Spanish

THE NEW TRAVELOCITY GUARANTEE

EVERYTHING YOU BOOK WILL BE RIGHT, OR WE'LL WORK WITH OUR TRAVEL PARTNERS TO MAKE IT RIGHT, RIGHT AWAY.

*To drive home the point,
we're going to use the word "right" in every single sentence.*

Let's get right to it. Right to the meat! Only Travelocity guarantees everything about your booking will be right, or we'll work with our travel partners to make it right, right away. Right on!

Here's a picture taken smack dab right in the middle of Antigua, where the guarantee also covers you.

The guarantee covers all but one of the items pictured to the right.

For example, what if the ocean view you booked actually looks out at a downright ugly parking lot? You'd be right to call – we're there for you. And no one in their right mind would be pleased to learn the rental car place has closed and left them stranded. Call Travelocity and we'll help get you back on the right track.

Now, you may be thinking, "Yeah, right, I'm so sure." That's OK; you have the right to remain skeptical. That is until we mention help is always right around the corner. Call us right off the bat, knowing that our customer service reps are there for you 24/7. Righting wrongs. Left and right.

Now if you're guessing there are some things we can't control, like the weather, well you're right. But we can help you with most things – to get all the details in righting,* visit **travelocity.com/guarantee**.

*Sorry, spelling things right is one of the few things not covered under the guarantee.

I'd give my right arm for a guarantee like this, although I'm glad I don't have to.

travelocity

You'll never roam alone.

IF YOU BOOK IT, IT SHOULD BE THERE.

Only Travelocity guarantees it will be, or we'll work with our travel partners to make it right, right away. So if you're missing a balcony or anything else you booked, just call us 24/7. **1-888-TRAVELOCITY.**

travelocit

You'll never roam al